The
City People's
Book of
Raising Food

The City People's Book of Raising Food

by
Helga & William Olkowski

Illustrations
by
Cathy Greene

Rodale Press Inc. / Book Division

Emmaus, Pennsylvania 18049

First Printing—March 1975

Library of Congress Cataloging in Publication Data

Olkowski, Helga.
   The city people's book of raising food.

Includes bibliographies and index.

1. Vegetable gardening. 2. Organic gardening. 3. Small animal culture. 4. City
and town life. I. Olkowski, William, joint author. II. Title.

SB321.04   635   75-2297
ISBN 0-87857-102-7
ISBN 0-87857-095-0 pbk.

The cover illustration of the Olkowskis'
house was done by Cathy Greene.

Book design by *Weidner Associates, Inc.*

OB-456

Contents

Chapter 9
MAKING FRIENDS WITH THE NEIGHBORS, OR ADVENTURES WITH CHICKENS, RABBITS, BEES, AND WORMS / 112

Chapter 10
MANAGING WILDLIFE IN THE URBAN GARDEN / 158

Introduction

I have always wanted to live on a farm. But I have always lived in the city. In this country, most people live in cities. In fact, all over the world, with a few exceptions, the trend is towards urbanization.

City people are a funny lot. They don't spend much time thinking about what keeps them alive—their life-support systems. There was a time when I didn't think about it much either. Oh, of course, I knew people need air to breathe, water to drink, and food to eat. But fresh air was obviously free and available and I didn't worry about the water that came through the pipes to my house, or the food that I bought at the store. If the vegetables and meats looked attractive, if they were á reasonable price, if they didn't look too hard to prepare, I bought them, took them home, prepared and ate them.

Well, we're all a bit more sophisticated now. We've heard about pesticide residues on foods, fertilizers contaminating water, lead in the air we breathe, the energy crisis, and other environmental disasters. If you are like me, you may have reached a point where the list is too long and upsetting to confront. You don't want to hear about another problem unless at the same time someone suggests what you can do about it. This is such a book—about the problem of producing food for city people and what you can do about it.

Consider the tomato. It takes large amounts of energy to produce the synthetic fertilizers used by the tomato farmer. Fossil fuels are heavily involved in modern agricultural technology and in the production of pesticides that such farming methods may seem to demand. Fossil fuel energy is also necessary to bring the tomato to the store where it is sold. How many of us walked home with our groceries this week? No doubt most used a car to bring the tomato to the kitchen, thus doing our bit directly toward energy consumption and air pollution, too.

And at the end of all that environmentally disastrous activity, what have we got? A tomato that hasn't seen the farm in many a day, a variety with a skin tough enough to withstand lots of mechanical handling, hopefully with pesticide residues below the FDA allowable tolerances. Nothing exactly to cheer about.

So what's a city person to do? Grow some of your own. I think that one can grow a good deal of food in the city, and have fun doing it. It was done during World War II— they were called Victory Gardens. The apartment dweller can grow tomatoes and cucumbers inside in a sunny window, citrus and bell peppers too. A window box salad, of loose-leaf lettuce, radishes, green onions, cress, baby carrots, and turnips, is a real possibility. There may be room for a planter box of food plants on the roof or in a courtyard, and even room to raise meat rabbits. You may be able to share a backyard or patio with a friend who has some outdoor space, or join forces with your neighbors in working on an empty lot, unused city-owned land; or you might talk your local parks and recreation people into letting you use a portion of a city park. Other city people have found a way. You can too.

Of course, not every city dweller wants to raise his own food. Even if you want to, you would have a hard time trying to raise all of it. But you can raise quite a lot. I know, because for the past four years my family has raised all of its own meat and vegetables in the middle of the city. We have taught hundreds of others to do the same. You can do it too. This book is to tell you how.

This is a record of some of our personal experiences and some of the "book learning" we found essential to our success. We hope it will be useful to you.

Helga Olkowski

P.S.: We've had a lot of help and encouragement from many friends and acquaintances, students, other teachers, and associates. To all these people whom we cannot thank individually we dedicate this book, but particularly to Drs. E. Williams, James Vlamis, and Bob Raabe, who helped us develop the Urban Garden Ecosystem class at the University of California; Tom Javits, who helped carry on the class and spread the word about city food growing; and all future urban gardeners.

chapter 1

We Start
Our Garden

We sat at the kitchen table one day, and Bill said, "Look at the world. The world is in bad shape." We started thinking about it. The more we thought, the worse we felt.

"If things fall apart, we're helpless," he said. Then, as they often will, Bill's thoughts drifted to his stomach. "What we need to do is grow our own food," he said.

"Where?" I asked nervously, peering out into our small backyard which at that time consisted mostly of a dying willow tree and two large, irregular holes. I had fancied having a Japanese garden out there. You know, with fish ponds, stepping stones, miniature trees, and all the things that could convert a space the size of a handkerchief into a vast panorama of unspoiled nature. About ten years prior, I had even gone so far as to dig holes for the ponds, and in a few unusually rainy years an inland sea had briefly materialized. Usually, however, the yard was distinguished mainly by a good crop of weeds.

"Forget the Japanese garden," Bill said. "We are going to turn the yard into a farm." The next thing I knew he had managed to locate our camping axe and was cutting down the willow tree.

Don't feel sorry. I did a little, but I was also relieved. That willow tree had taught me a valuable lesson. I had bought it once on an impulse, while touring a nursery in the hot, central valley of California, far from where I live on cool, foggy San Francisco Bay. A variety unsuited to my own climate, it soon succumbed to a fungus which was slowly killing it. Plants out of their native area are frequently stressed and are more susceptible to the different and strange organisms of other regions.

Once the tree was down, and as much as possible of the root system removed, we surveyed our little plot. It is long and narrow, running north and south, bounded by a two story apartment house on the east and our own three story castle on the west. Not too promising, presenting the typical problems of a city garden—not very much space, not very much light. We are typical city dwellers too, not having much time to give to farming. Both of us are working full time, coming home to supper tired, with only a little daylight left. Weekends are busy with preparing lectures and reading papers.

"I believe in building winning situations," Bill said. "Let's start small!" And so we did. Allowing for the shade cast by the fence and hedge along the south side of the lot, with a digging fork we turned over the dirt in the small area we thought would get the most hours of sun during the day.

In a way we were complete beginners. I had done quite a bit of ornamental gardening before (mainly in the *front* of the house, so as to create a nice impression when one came up the walk) but not much food raising. The botany I had studied in college didn't seem very helpful now. I felt really ignorant. I didn't know what to plant where. What could stand partial shade? The soil seemed like a clay out of which you could make pottery. We guessed the plants might find it pretty tough going but we didn't know how to improve it. My father said, "Anything that can grow weeds that tall *must* be pretty rich soil." But we didn't know how to tell what it had and what it lacked.

We did something very inconsistent with both our temperaments, I guess; we turned to books first. We read and read and read. We found out that most of the really scientific, comprehensive texts on raising food were aimed at farmers, people who had large machines and large fields with plenty of all-day sun, who could put their full attention on agriculture. No one wrote specifically about raising food in the city—urbagriculture! We started visiting other city food gardens and talking with everyone interested and experienced.

The city is a special place. For intensive food production, particularly small urban meat-producing systems, you need special information. It was hard to come by a lot of it. A good deal we learned by trial and error. Each evening, when we sat down at the supper table we would ask each other, "Now what are we eating tonight that we didn't produce ourselves, but might in the future?" We wanted to prove we could do it.

"If we are successful at this," Bill said, "we'll teach all our students. We'll write a book telling everyone how we did it. We can create a new agriculture, a new awakening to the values and pleasures of contact with the soil, plants, and animals that support us. We could also get to see lots of beetles, butterflies, flies, and other microwildlife." (Bill is one of those curious people called entomologists, who likes bugs!)

chapter 2

Urban Eden? or.
What's So Special
About the City?

Where can you find plants and animals from every continent on earth, all in one place? Why, in the city, of course.

People feel nostalgia for the landscapes of their youth. The first settlers brought over their favorite plants from the old world. Many became weeds and fast crowded out the natives. When the settlers moved west, they brought eastern species with them. My California city has German lindens and New England tulip trees rubbing elbows with native walnuts.

People like exotic plants too. There are avid cactus growers in rainy Seattle and rainforest fern lovers in arid Tucson. There's a challenge in growing a plant in an environment foreign to it. Most of our food crops come from somewhere else; so do many of the bugs and other animals that eat them. Knowing something about the original environment of a plant may give you a clue as to its particular requirements. Putting plants together in a very small space, when they need different kinds of care, can be a real challenge too.

Besides the scarcity of open space for growing food, the less than perfect light conditions on what space there is, and the exotic nature of the plants and animals, several other characteristics make the city a special place: the disturbed soils, for example.

When digging foundations for a house, laying sewer lines, and grading for walkways and streets, the original topsoil may be carted off or buried, and the natural surface drainage impeded. Infertile subsoil may be exposed or miscellaneous debris left behind by the builders. The teaching garden we eventually developed in town for students at the University of California is a virtual treasure trove of old door handles, nuts and bolts, and pieces of glass. While the latter may be the most immediately hazardous to the gardener, the loss of fertile topsoil is a more serious problem in terms of the efforts needed to remedy the situation.

Whatever else they may be, the density of people and vehicles assures that city soils are compacted. They are also exposed to a variety of pollutants, as are the plants themselves. For instance, both the soils and exposed portions of the plants may accumulate lead from automobile gasoline. Next to a very busy intersection, particularly on the windward side, greens like spinach and lettuce may receive quite a dose of lead, while below-ground beets, turnips, and carrots, or peas within their protecting pods, may remain unaffected.

Away from heavy traffic lead may not pose a problem, but there may be other noticeable effects from man-made pollution. Some air pollutants act mainly to retard the growth of plants, occasionally causing striking symptoms of plant injury which may be confused with disease or mineral deficiencies, but do not make the plants unsafe to eat. For details about these less desirable random inputs into the urban ecosystem you may want to see the good color photographs in the booklet *Air Pollution Injury to Vegetations*, by the U.S. Department of Health, Education and Welfare. It is available from the Government Printing Office in Washington, D. C. Incidentally, many of the test plants pictured in the book were grown outdoors in cities like New York or Los Angeles. Lucky readers who live in communities that are deliberately controlling their growth and auto traffic!

But with all its special problems, urbagriculture has its advantages too. Cities are usually warmer than the surrounding country, so you may be able to plant earlier and harvest longer than the farmer. Growing food on a small scale means that many simple, cheap, environmentally sound, but labor-intensive methods are practical. You can create minienvironments, manage insect populations, fertilize and improve the structure of your soil with methods not usually economical for the large scale farmer. Using compost at the rate of forty tons to an acre is possible if you have only one thousandth of an acre!

In the city we live in the midst of abundant resources, unused and unwanted by less conservation-minded folk. Leaves from the city trees on their way to the dump, scrap lumber, and empty five-gallon cans cast-off in the industrial and commercial areas, abundant greens from the outsides of vegetables, or those too ripe or unesthetic to sell, thrown away at the supermarket, hair sweepings from the barber shop, sawdust from the cabinet makers—these are only a few of the wonderful raw materials available free and nearby for the urban farm. It's like living in the Garden of Eden. Well, almost.

chapter 3

Doing the Best
with Where You Are

Climate, Microclimate, and Miniclimate

Some like it cold, some like it hot.

When we put in our first vegetable garden we set out plenty of chard. It is a vegetable that grows well all year 'round in Berkeley's moderate "Mediterranean" climate. But you may be gardening in Minneapolis, Minnesota or Gainesville, Florida. Climate will affect *what* you can plant *when*.

The climate of your area is a summary of your daily weather during the year. The word "climate" usually refers to a large region like the eastern seaboard, the Great Lakes states, or the southern Rockies.

Your own city probably has a microclimate which differs a little from the general climate of the whole area. Besides higher temperatures than the surrounding country (it may be *much* hotter in the summer in high density neighborhoods with all the energy used to run air conditioners and the heat expelled by them into the air outdoors), your city will be affected by local geography. Perhaps it is bordered by a large body of water with its moderating influence, or sheltered from cold winds by a range of hills. Lots of particulate matter in the air from industry may mean more overcast days or may affect the pattern of rainfall over the city.

Although there is a saying that no one does much about the weather, in fact modern industrial man (that means you and me, friend) has been affecting it a good deal and most of it by accident. The Massachusetts Institute of Technology held a conference on the subject, and the papers are published in a fascinating book called *Inadvertent Climate Modification*, available from MIT Press, Cambridge, Massachusetts.

But what the urban farmer wants to know is, how can one affect the weather deliberately and for positive results? The factors you need to consider are temperature, moisture, light, and wind. The general climate of your city will be affected by such considerations as latitude and elevation (you can expect roughly a one-degree rise in temperature with each 300-feet rise in elevation). The distance you are from the coasts or other large bodies of water, the topography of the region, the prevailing winds—none of these can you change.

The weather you *can* affect is the miniclimate, the climate unique to your own backyard. Russell Beatty, in the Environmental Horticulture Department at the University of California, Berkeley, helped us greatly in organizing our ideas regarding urban miniclimate modification. He would begin his lectures on the subject by asking two questions: 1) How can the microclimate of a plant be manipulated to increase plant survival? 2) How can plants be manipulated to affect the microclimate?

Let us consider the various factors one by one and see what you can do about them. First there is temperature. This is the most critical in terms of growing plants and often the most difficult to affect. For one thing, it is the extremes of temperature that make the most difference.

Temperature

What plants can take cool weather? This means early spring for many parts of the country, and wintertime for the California Coast and southern states. Chard can, as we mentioned before, and beets, which are closely related. Also peas, fava beans (which are really a pea, not a bean, and are also called horsebeans), spinach, lettuce, carrots, potatoes, and all the brassicas, that is, turnips, rutabagas, radishes, cabbages, cauliflower, broccoli, Brussels sprouts, kohlrabi, mustard greens, collards, kale, and any other members of this large family that you may be fond of and we've forgotten to mention.

Some brassicas, like collards, can even take a light frost, and it is a frost, temperatures from 32° to 30° F, that really is our main concern. A plant's ability to withstand cold temperatures is called "hardiness." Gradually getting plants used to the cold is called "hardening off." This is what we do when we take a seedling grown indoors on the windowsill and move it to the semi-cool porch for a few days before transplanting it out into the garden itself.

Root crops like carrots and parsnips can be left in the ground fully grown when winter comes if they are protected from low temperatures by a deep insulating blanket of compost or straw and then a covering of snow. Trunks of trees and shrubs can be protected with straw jackets for prolonged cold spells. The problem is frosts that come when the plants are in an actively growing state, in the late spring and early fall.

The kind easiest to protect against are called "radiation" frosts because the heat from the sun that is stored by the earth during the day is lost, or radiated, to the outer atmosphere at night. This happens on very still, clear nights, when no clouds are present to reflect the heat waves back toward the earth, and no wind mixes the warm and cool air. Moisture in the air is also a protection from this kind of cold, so you can expect more problems with radiation frosts if your city is not under the influence of a marine atmosphere.

Plan ahead to protect your cool weather crops from radiation frosts by doing your earliest plantings close to the house where eaves or other overhanging structures may reradiate the heat back down to the plants. Here is where you can turn your city environment to your advantage. A south wall may store heat and give it out at night. Benedictine and Cistercian monks knew this and thus were able to grow heat-loving fruits far north in medieval England by pruning the trees and vines flat against the walls of their gardens.

One of our early steps in designing our urban garden was to take advantage of the extra heat along the south wall of our house. We decided to build raised beds there for several reasons. First of all, it is a scant six feet to the edge of the property and a high bamboo hedge we grow to give us privacy on that side. Except for midsummer, plants low on

cut-away side view of narrow, raised bed along house.

the ground there would always be in the shade of that hedge. Secondly, any plants we set in the soil would be directly competing with the roots of the hedge. Furthermore, the drainage in the area is very poor and during our winter rains only large board planks make the walkway passable.

Our solution was a long, narrow eighteen-inch raised bed, flat against the house. First we built a cement barrier to keep the soil away from the stucco walls (and keep out termites), then we built brick retaining walls to hold our planting mixture. We used sifted dirt from where we constructed our chicken house, mixed with compost and a little sand to lighten the very heavy clay. Then, flat against the house wall we stretched fencing to tie tomato plants to and on which vines might climb. Since all we have is vertical space the plants would have to be encouraged to grow upwards. Here in this narrow, unlikely spot, winter and cold-spring peas have flourished and tomatoes and lemon cucumbers have survived late into the fall.

Another strategy is to make your early vegetables portable. Five-gallon containers can be moved under trees or other protection if you suspect a frost coming—we'll talk about container gardening in a later section of this book.

A cardboard box or bushel basket, inverted over the plant for the night, will also help. It should be large enough so the leaves do not press against the inside of the top. Remember, it is the heat stored in the soil you wish to trap. Wrapping a bag or cloth around the plant and tying it around the stem will not offer protection from this kind of frost.

When planning your urban garden, take into consideration that cold air is denser, heavier, and flows down to the lowest spot. Walls, fences, and borders of low shrubs can block cold air or channel it to flow around a low planting area. Large planter boxes on our porch have given us our best crops of cool weather vegetables. The angle of the sun is such that they receive light during the short days of the year where the same area is shaded by the porch roof in the summer. The few feet of elevation give the plants a temperature advantage, and the porch roof reflects back the heat at night. It may be pouring, or dark in the garden, but lettuce for our lunch sandwiches is always conveniently available.

If an unexpected frost seems imminent and the vegetables can't be moved or covered, then lightly sprinkling them during the freezing hours may save the day. Since water releases heat as it turns to ice, the constant freezing of a fine spray of water may create enough heat to keep the plants undamaged. This method is used by commercial lettuce growers in California when rare winter frosts are expected, but the disadvantage is that you must keep sprinklers going all during the danger period. A timer set to start the sprinkler during the coldest hours of the night and early morning should do the trick. All in all, though, this is just an emergency method.

One of the oldest and most successful ways to raise the temperature and extend the season is by using cold frames, hotbeds, minigreenhouses, or cloches—small portable glass or plastic shelters.

The principle of the greenhouse is that light rays from the sun pass easily through the glass or plastic (although only certain plastics pass all of the spectrum most useful to plants). Once they strike the ground or other surfaces they are converted to infrared (the same as the heat waves given off by animals and plants themselves); in this form they do not pass back to the atmosphere as readily, thus are trapped inside. A useful model we devised, after seeing pictures of similar structures used in Israel, consisted of a series of wire or split bamboo arches placed over the bed to be protected and shoved into the ground far enough (six inches or so) to stay put. A plastic sheet is spread over this and a second series of arches placed over the first to hold the plastic in place. These tube-shelters are open at both

*plastic secured between bamboo strips
to form small, temporary greenhouse*

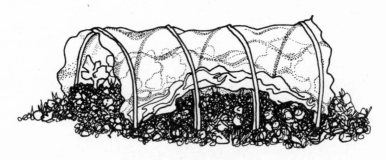

plastic greenhouse with side rolled up

ends for ventilation so they should be placed at right angles to the wind for greatest warmth inside. Additional ventilation may be obtained very easily, if necessary, by pulling the plastic up a few inches from the ground on the north side, whenever needed. The main difficulty with all such minishelters is that they may become too moist inside and encourage the growth of disease-inducing fungi. These shelters can be as long as you like, but less than six feet does not seem to give enough of a warming effect.

That windbreaks alone will help plants survive and grow during cold weather became apparent with our use of the above-described shelter. As an experiment, we set up the shelter at right angles to the wind and then planted identical-sized broccoli plants within and on both sides. Those within the shelter rapidly became triple the size of those exposed on the side toward the wind. Those on the protected side did not show the impressive growth difference of those inside, but did grow faster and larger than those to the windward. Of course, many more elaborate and lasting cloches or minishelters can be constructed. We recommend ours because it is so simple and inexpensive.

heat trapped by container to protect young seedling

With some plants, it is not having *enough* cold weather, or *cold* enough weather, that becomes a problem. Many fruit trees require a certain number of hours below 45° F. It is difficult to get them to bear fruit in areas of the country that have mild winters. Finding the best varieties of the foods you want to grow for the extremes of climate that your city experiences, as well as the length of the growing period, is an adventure we'll talk about a little later.

What about the other extreme—hot weather? Beans, corn, cucumbers, squashes, tomatoes, peppers, eggplants, and okra are examples of vegetables that demand the heat. This may mean pulling back the mulch and letting the soil thoroughly warm up before setting out seeds or seedlings. A dark covering on the soil—tarpaper or plastic (though we hate to recommend it because it is made from nonrenewable fossil fuels and creates a waste problem when you are through with it because it cannot be composted)—helps to increase the heat absorption of the soil. Good drainage is important too, since wet soils take longer to warm up.

The general range of temperatures that are comfortable for man, 65° to 88° F, is comfortable for plants too. Although they may grow vigorously from 50° to 107° F, photosynthesis, or the making of sugar in the plant, begins to decline above 87° F. Plant tissues may be killed at 127° F, but they may show signs of heat stress well below that point. Although they take in water faster in warm weather, plants lose water more quickly then, too. The drier the air, the more the wind blows away the layer of saturated air close to the leaves, and the faster the plant will lose water, until a point may be reached when the roots can't take it in fast enough and the plant wilts.

Besides wilting, plants may show a brown scorch along the leaf margin and the tip, or a yellowing that indicates the chlorophyll has been damaged. However, these symptoms may also be signs of mineral deficiencies (yellowing indicates lack of nitrogen or sulphur), or salt build-up (brown margins) usually associated with insufficient moisture. Obviously, you need to be sensitive to all the elements necessary to good plant growth. Although we might talk about them one by one in a book like this, in the real environment they interact.

Various plants have different ways to cope with high temperatures: the arrangement of the leaves—those held perpendicular to the sun do not absorb as much heat; through coloration—gray-green foliage is sun tolerant but cannot handle low light intensities; thick wax layers of cutin on the leaf surfaces which insulate, reflect heat, and prevent excessive water loss; and hairs on the leaf itself which offer shade. Cacti, with their many spines, carry their own lathe houses with them, so to speak.

One can provide shade for heat-sensitive plants like lettuce and spinach by suspending shade cloth over them. This is sold in varying degrees of transparency. Lathe shelters give good protection—the boards should run north and south so that each spot on the plants is alternately exposed to sun and shade. Container plants can be moved under tree canopies. Heat-sensitive plants can be planted on the east side of structures so that they catch the morning sun but afternoon shade. In general, the south to southwest side of any structure is the area for your heat-loving plants.

Wind

Wind and moisture have interconnected effects that are easy to understand—the moving air replaces the more moist layer close to the leaf surface, thus having a drying effect upon the plants. The wind also reduces the temperature of the leaves. An increase in wind speed of three miles per hour may reduce air temperatures $3°$ F; and the windier it is, the more closely the leaf temperature will approach air temperature. Transpiration of water through the leaves is one of the important ways that plants can cool themselves.

Good air circulation is particularly important in preventing the build-up of certain kinds of plant diseases. Pruning a plant so that air and light can reach the interior, and spacing plants so that air can circulate freely will help control humidity. Of course, it is partly this water vapor transpired from the plants that makes vegetation in covered areas pleasant to human beings and a grassy tree-covered park a welcome relief from asphalt and cement. Soil humidity can be managed through your watering techniques, the use of raised beds, and the addition of organic material to the soil and on top of it as a mulch—more about all this when we get to the subject of soils.

Where wind is a problem because of its chilling or drying effects, screens may be effective. It is important that wind-breaks be partially penetrable; actually about 30 to 50 percent is best. Solid barriers tend to increase the gusts and turbulence on the leeward side. Thus a basketweave or similar style fence with open spaces is superior to a solid one, and shrubs and trees are better yet. On level ground a plant barrier will reduce winds for a distance roughly five times its height—the greatest protection being close to the barrier itself.

Light

Light intensity can be affected by pruning and spacing of plants. Walls and other structures painted white will help reflect light, too. Various urban dwellers, plagued with small spaces shaded by nearby structures, have tried many ingenious devices such as mirrors and aluminum foil reflectors to brighten shady areas, but none is an adequate substitute for sunlight. A rough rule of thumb is: plants from which you eat the leaves (lettuce, spinach, chard, etc.) can stand the most shade, those from which you eat the fruits (tomatoes, squashes, corn, etc.) need the most sun, and root crops fall somewhere in between.

Those areas that get no direct sun at all—the north side of a tall house or fence, the garage or basement—are suitable only for raising mushrooms, meat, earthworms for feeding chickens, or for the composting system.

Mushrooms can be, actually should be, grown without light, but we want to interject some words of caution: the directions that come along with mushroom spawn you can buy imply that it is simple to grow mushrooms at home. Not so. It is very tricky to maintain the proper humidity and temperature (a cave will do nicely), and process the compost medium on which the spawn is to be grown. It must be warm while the spawn is spreading through the beds, and cold while the mushrooms are being harvested. Before you go into it, we suggest you do some additional reading on the subject and be sure you are willing to take the time and trouble and can provide the proper environments.

Rabbits and chickens can both be raised without direct sun. More about this in Chapter 9.

Light conditions may affect what you plant when, as well as where you plant it, just as temperature does. The shortening days of late summer, the lengthening days of spring, may each have a different and specific effect upon a plant. The result may be similar to the way excess heat can cause spinach or lettuce to "bolt," that is, prematurely form flowers and seeds, becoming rather tough, sometimes bitter, and usually inedible in the process.

Want to plant Chinese cabbage in the summer, or an onion that forms large bulbs in your area? The answer is to select a variety suitable to your latitude and time of year. Some vegetables are indifferent, but others cannot be grown at just any time. A great favorite of ours, coriander, which we love raw in salads and cooked in Chinese dishes, is strictly a spring and early summer vegetable in the San Francisco area. During the late summer no sooner does it reach picking stage than it goes to seed, though the temperatures remain nearly the same in July as they were in June.

How to tell which varieties of onions, Chinese cabbage, or other vegetables are suitable for spring or fall? The seed catalogues are sources of information; so are your state agricultural experiment station and county farm advisor. So are others growing food in your own city. How to find and meet them? Local garden clubs or ecology centers may know who's growing their own food. The letters to the editor section of *Organic Gardening and Farming* magazine may put you in touch with other urban or suburban farmers in your area.

So, with these observations about microclimate in mind, take a look at the areas where you hope to grow some food, and see how they stack up. Don't forget to include in your calculations the height of the sun in the sky at different times of the year and how that will change the position of shadows from adjacent buildings. You may find, as we did, that during some parts of the year only the roof gets enough light to produce the vegetables you want. Your sunniest spot may require some wind protection.

Now, having picked where you will start your food production, and considered what modifications you may need to make for wind, frost, or sun protection, take a look at the soil.

chapter 4

What's So Great About Just Plain Dirt?

Recently, in an urban food-growing class, a student who had been listening patiently to discussions about soil cultivation asked, "What's so special about dirt? Wouldn't it be easier for city gardeners to avoid messing with it altogether and just grow plants hydroponically?" She went on to describe a visit she had with friends who grow all their vegetables that way; that is, in water, adding nutrients as needed. This student proclaimed them as tasty as any other. Perhaps some people feel that it is cleaner, neater, more modern not to have to mess around with nasty old dirt.

Now first of all, we must point out to you that dirt, as our soil professor, Dr. Williams, was fond of saying, is something you get under your fingernails. What you grow plants in is "soil." Why bother with soil? Well, for one thing, growing plants in water takes a great deal of energy. Artificial nutrients must be added to the water, and the synthetic fertilizers take energy to produce (especially natural gas, already in short supply). Since roots need oxygen, energy may be used to pump air into the water. Should the water become stagnant, the plants will soon begin to rot.

In addition to the energy input you will need to devise some means of holding the plants up. In greenhouses, plants such as tomatoes or cucumbers may be supported on strings or trellises attached to the ceiling. Gravel, sawdust, or sand is used in some hydroponic systems so the roots have something to hang on to. Soil, on the other hand, provides a medium in which plants can support themselves—and it has some other wonderful qualities as well. It is a matrix for plant nutrient exchanges between the surfaces of clay particles, the soil-water solution, and plant roots; gas exchanges between air and plant roots; water storage for plants; and last but not least, an environment for soil life—the decomposers and detritivores. Most important: soil contains many nutrients which would be costly to replace.

When we started our urban farm, one of our first tasks was to learn what soil is, besides something underfoot we had been taking for granted.

How Soil Happens

Before the city was built, there was the land. There was the earth—rocks, water, sun, wind, plants, animals, and microorganisms living here. These, all together, developed the soil. Then the city was started and gradually the soil was affected by the weight of heavy things being moved across it and the addition of man-made debris.

Below the soil everywhere are rocks. In some places the soil is very deep. In other areas, the parent rocks of the soil are very close to the surface. Rocks can be described in many ways.

Sometimes it is useful to classify them according to the way they were formed. There are rocks that cooled directly from molten material, called "igneous" rocks. Agni was the Indo-European god of fire, and the name is still honored in our words "ignition" and "ignite."

If this molten material cooled slowly, the minerals in it formed big crystals, the way sugar crystals form slowly around a string when you make rock candy. Granite is such a rock. If the material cools quickly, for example underwater or close to the surface of the ground, the crystals will be small. Sometimes they will not even have time to form, and a glassy rock-like obsidian, much favored by the Indians for making arrowheads, will be the result.

There are other groups of rocks that are nothing more than the compressed accumulations of sediments—particles of other rocks that have been broken down by the action of wind, water, and temperature changes. These "sedimentary" rocks may be sandstones, for instance, if they are composed of evenly worn materials on land; shales and mudstones if they were formed of finer materials along the edges of a lake; or limestones full of the dead skeletons of marine animals if they were formed beneath oceans.

The third general classification of rocks is the "metamorphic," which means "changed." When any rocks, regardless of their origin, are buried deeply in the earth and subjected to great heat and pressure, they undergo characteristic changes. They become harder, denser, and often the minerals in the rocks will line themselves up in bands or striations. Thus, granites may become shists or gneisses with lovely stripes, limestones become marbles, shales become slate, and so on.

These many varieties of rocks are composed of different minerals, most of them made up of different chemical compounds. Slowly, the surfaces of these rocks are broken down into soil through the process called weathering. Physically the rocks may be weathered through abrasion by ice or wind and water carrying sand particles, the same way the windshield of a car can become worn and pitted in a dust storm. Temperature changes will also cause the rocks to crack and split off small pieces. Chemical weathering is important also. Rain water, falling through the air, picks up carbon dioxide and becomes a weak acid, carbonic acid, which will start chemical changes in the minerals composing the rocks. Plants exude organic acids from their roots which also help in this process of soil building.

The kind of soil that results after weathering will depend on: the original rock, or parent material, including the particular minerals it contains; the climate under which the decomposing takes place, that is, the rainfall, temperature, and wind conditions; the slope of the land where the soil is forming; the length of time the process has been going on; and most important, the kind of plants that are growing there.

For an excellent introduction to this subject, see *The Soils That Support Us*, by Charles E. Kellogg. In his book, Kellogg gives a description of this action of plants influencing the kind of soil that is formed. He contrasts two areas of different rainfall and temperatures: places where tall grasses are native, and forests of pines and spruces. The tall grasses feed heavily on those chemicals in the soil called bases—calcium, magnesium, and potassium. Then, as the abundant grass tops die and decompose, these bases are released at the surface, preventing the soil from becoming acid, even if rainfall is plentiful. In contrast, pines and spruces feed very lightly on the bases and return very little organic matter to the soil. These more acid materials will decompose very slowly, in part because of the many complex resins and oils they contain. However, the rate of decomposition is always faster in warm weather. Thus the same conifers may have thick mats under them in the north, while warmer southern soils may be more quickly depleted of their organic matter.

Bacteria do not grow well in acid soils, leaving decomposition primarily to the fungi. Fungi produce rather soluble materials which are leached (washed down) easily from the soil by water. Bacteria, on the other hand, which do best in neutral soil, produce compounds that are less soluble. These less soluble minerals then remain in the upper soil long enough to be available to plant roots once again. So neutral soil, where abundant organic matter is decomposed by bacteria, tends to be more naturally rich in available plant nutrients.

When you take into account all these complex, varying

conditions, you can see there is no such thing as a "normal" soil. There are thousands of kinds of soils in the world. Because of all the factors involved, different soil may be developed from the same parent rock and similar soils may be developed from different original materials. But if the original rocks never had a certain mineral, calcium, for instance, as is the case with serpentine rocks common along the northern California coast, then the soils will be lacking in it also. Luckily, city gardeners deal with an area so small in size they are often able to make even the poorest, most deficient soil productive, while the intensive care that this requires would not be economically feasible to a farmer working on a larger scale.

To sum it up: rocks are broken *down* by weathering, but then soil is built *up* by plants and microorganisms. Different proportions of minerals from different depths in the ground are deposited by plants at the surface when they die. Then different microorganisms decompose the materials at different rates depending upon different conditions. No wonder soils are different!

Three quarters of the earth's surface is water. Of the one fourth that is land, a little less than half is too steep or too dry for growing crops. The little that remains is what supports all humanity. Since the best agricultural land is generally the flattest land, it is also the most attractive for building. Here in California, which still produces a large percentage of the nation's foods, the finest, deepest soils in the world are slowly disappearing under freeways, shopping centers, houses, and all the other structures of suburban sprawl. It may take more than 1,000 years to produce an inch of fertile topsoil, its fertility being in great measure dependent on the amount of life and organic matter it contains. Construction of roads or buildings usually removes this topsoil or mixes it with infertile subsoil and compacts it, destroying its structure. It will take more than tearing up the asphalt and adding a few synthesized fertilizers to restore those destroyed soils to productive agricultural use again.

Soil Character

Looked at poetically, every soil has a personality. It has a history, as we have just seen, and it also has a profile, a texture, and a structure. The personality of your soil needs to be accounted for when you cultivate, water, and fertilize.

The soil profile is a description of how the layers of the soil differ as you go deeper and deeper, from the surface down to the rock underneath. On top lies the undecomposed organic matter and beneath that the materials that have been broken down already by the action of microorganisms and larger animals. In our garden, we give a lot of attention to this layer by producing compost and laying it on top of the soil as a mulch. The idea is to copy the natural process as it would occur in a forest, prairie, or wherever plants exist.

Below this layer begins the topsoil. This is the layer with the most organic matter, oxygen, and living organisms, including plant roots. This layer will often be darker than the soil below it. It is also the area from which the minerals are leached away by the action of water moving down because of the pull of gravity. The topsoil is the most fertile, valuable part of the soil profile and the one most easily destroyed by ignorance and carelessness.

Beneath the topsoil comes the subsoil. Here the minerals carried down by water may be deposited. If you dig a hole in your own yard exposing the layers of soil, or if you are studying these layers in a road cut where you can see them easily, you can often recognize this layer by poking at it with a penknife. Starting at the top, pick away at each visible layer; when you come to a hard area, you can guess that's where the minerals have been deposited.

Sometimes, in fact, this layer may be so dense that plant roots and drainage water have a hard time making it through. This type of layer is called a "hard pan" by soil scientists. If the hard pan is severe, you may need to cultivate deeply to break it up. Besides forming naturally through mineral deposition, hard pans may also be caused by always plowing to the same depth and destroying the structure of the soil by the shearing action of the plow blade. If your house has been built upon soil originally used for mechanized agriculture you may have inherited such a "plow pan."

Of course, one can be fooled when reading a soil profile. In our student garden we dug a hole in the process of creating some experimental fish ponds. The top layer was the blackest, changing gradually to pale yellow subsoil. Then, surprise, there was another dark layer below that! The mystery was cleared up when we learned something of the history of that area. Apparently, the original fertile topsoil had been buried when the surrounding streets had first been laid, the entire end of the block being leveled and then topsoil from somewhere else spread over it. Topsoil may also be transported by streams and glaciers as well as man, and thus may not always be derived from the rock found below it.

How close the rock is to the surface of your land will dictate in part whether you will need to resort to building a growing medium on top or whether you are lucky enough to have many feet of rich well-drained soils, as are found in some of California's productive agricultural valleys.

Soil Texture

The proportion of sand, silt, and clay particles in your soil determines its *texture*. Classified by size, the sand particles are the largest—usually easily visible to the naked eye. Silt particles are finer—like sifted cake flour. Clay particles are the smallest of all—too fine to be seen individually without an electron microscope. Silts are often wind-blown materials, powdery when dry and greasy when wet. The sand and silt particles have usually been altered in little besides size, compared to the rocks from which they were derived. Clay, on the other hand, has usually undergone chemical changes which, in addition to the very small size of the individual particles, gives it special qualities. Most of us are familiar with the nature of clay from having made things with it when we were small, or from trying to clean it off our boots when we've gone walking through a muddy field.

In ordinary speech, the word "loam" is used to mean any good soil. To a soil scientist the term has a very precise meaning—referring to a particular mixture of silt, sand, and clay.

Now, the two questions that came to our minds when we first learned about all this, were 1. How can I tell what my soil texture is? and 2. Why does it matter?

A Touch Test for Your Soil

1. Take a bit of soil into the palm of one hand—a tablespoon full or a little less.

2. Add a little water (you can even use spit).

3. With the fingers of the other hand work the water into the soil so that it is thoroughly wet, but don't use so much water that the mixture is runny. It should be quite firm.

Now try two tests.

1. Rub the mixture out thinly against your palm. What do you feel and see? Clay gives the soil a shine when you press down firmly and spread it out. It feels slippery. If the soil is sandy, there will be no shine. It will feel gritty—you may be able to feel individual sand grains. Take the time to

mix and knead the soil thoroughly, because clay takes a while to wet through. You can be deceived into thinking you are feeling sand particles, when really they are small hard clay lumps that haven't yet softened. Silt gives the soil a greasy quality, but will not make it plastic the way clay does.

2. Roll the wet soil into a ball, then into as long and thin a snake as possible. Let the last inch or so of the snake stick out over the edge of your palm. If you can, pick up the snake roll by one end. The sandier the soil is, the harder time you will have getting it rolled into a ball, and any snake you manage to shape will quickly fall apart. As the percentage of clay increases, you will be able to roll a thick snake that keeps its shape, but if the end protrudes beyond the edge of your hand it will be apt to crack and break off. The more clay, the thinner the snake you can roll, until with a high percentage of clay, you can roll a very thin strip that will hold together when you pick up one end. (When the amount of clay in the soil reaches approximately 35 percent or more, a snake 1/4 inch in diameter can be picked up by one end without breaking.)

Learning to tell the texture, or proportion of sand, silt, and clay of your soil by this method takes practice. It is like training your ear to recognize different notes of the scale—a comparison with other notes is helpful. You need to try this touch test with many soils and see how they differ. Wherever you go, take a bit of soil into your hand and try it out, while remembering the ones you've worked before. (Your friends will get used to seeing you kneading little balls of damp soil while staring reflectively off into space with a faraway look on your face.)

Why Does Texture Matter?

At this point you are probably thinking, "Why bother?" The answer is, because the amount of sand, silt, and clay influences water movement *through* soil, the amount of water *held* by the soil, and whether or not the nutrients the plants need, many of which come from decaying organic materials, will be held in the soil available to the plant roots. What it comes down to is, clay is "where the action is" in soils, in relation to water and to the minerals that plants need.

We were very surprised when we first learned this. We had been dismayed to discover the soil in our backyard was such heavy clay that when wet, it felt as if you might mold pottery out of it, and when dry, deep cracks would appear. Then we learned that the chemical weathering that clays have undergone and their very small size are responsible for two valuable properties. Each tiny clay platelet is flat and thin, giving it a tremendous surface area relative to its volume. It is also negatively charged. This means that clays can attract, retain, and exchange the positively charged minerals that are necessary for plant growth. In a sandy soil the same plant nutrients will wash right through with every rain or irrigation. It also means that clays retain water very well on their surfaces and in the many tiny spaces between particles.

These clay platelets are like microscopic sandwiches, made up of thin layers of silica and alumina. Some clays actually absorb water between the layers, causing them to swell when wet and shrink when dry—thus the deep cracks that used to appear suddenly everywhere in our garden. (But not any more: I'll tell you what we did when we come to considering soil structure.)

To sum it up, then, the texture, or proportion of sand, silt, and clay in your soil, determines how and when you water, fertilize, and cultivate.

What does the texture of your soil have to do with watering your garden?

In clay or heavy soils, water infiltrates very slowly after rain or irrigation because the spaces between the particles are very small. As they begin to absorb water, the clay platelets may swell and further impede water movement. Water rises very slowly by capillary action from the underground water table, and it may rise as high as six feet (capillary action is the upward movement of water in small spaces due to the mutual attraction of the soil and the water).

So, with clay soils you need to water a *great deal* to wet the soil to a good depth, but you don't need to water very often.

In sandy or light soils, water infiltrates very quickly, but the soil dries out quickly too, as water moves down by the pull of gravity. Water will rise very quickly from the water table, but it will not rise very high, leveling off at about eighteen inches.

So, with sandy soils you don't need to add a lot of water each time, but you need to water frequently.

Clay soils can really hold more water than sandy ones—about one and a half gallons of water for every cubic foot of soil, compared to only half a gallon in the same amount of sandy soil. This works out to just under an inch of water to wet a foot deep in sandy soils, but almost two and a half inches of water to wet the same distance down in a clay soil.

The way we tested our sprinkler to find out how long it took to deliver an inch of water was to set out a series of one-pound coffee cans at progressively greater distances from the center to the edge of the area it watered, and we timed how long it took to fill the cans an inch deep. This method will also tell you whether your sprinkler is delivering water evenly from the center out, or if some areas are getting waterlogged while others are still thirsty.

The depth from which a plant will normally extract water varies greatly with the kind of plant it is as well as the structure of the soil and how easily the roots can penetrate it. In general, though, the main root zone for lawn grasses and leafy vegetables is the top one foot; for corn, tomatoes, and small shrubs the top one to two feet; and for small trees and large shrubs the top two or three feet. Some large trees go down twenty to thirty feet. Exceptions do occur; for example, alfalfa in loose soil could go down thirty feet.

Water is lost from this root zone when it percolates downward through the pull of gravity, and it is also lost by evaporation from the surface of the soil. How much is lost how fast depends on the wind velocity and the temperature of the air. Warm air can hold more moisture than cool air, and if the saturated air is blown away from the surface of the ground, more can evaporate into the unsaturated air which takes its place. The way we handle this situation in our garden is to cover all exposed earth between plants with mulch.

Mulching

Compost is the ideal mulch. It provides a habitat for many animals that live on decaying matter. Some, such as earwigs which are also carnivorous (meaning they'll eat some of your pest insects as well as eat plant matter) and sowbugs or pillbugs, actually cause less damage to growing plants when there is plenty of organic mulch around. Another reason for using compost on top of the soil is that it breaks the fall of raindrops, preventing them from eroding away the sides of raised beds, and pounding the surface of the ground, creating a hard crust. Little seedlings have no trouble poking their way through a soil surface kept soft, moist, and at an even temperature by a layer of compost. Another advantage of using a compost mulch is that as the material decomposes, the nutrients and sometimes larger, not-completely-decomposed pieces are carried down into the ground by water and various animals, such as earthworms.

However, other mulches can be just as effective in reducing water loss by evaporation from the open soil. Since Berkeley has rather cool summers by comparison with much of the rest of the country, we sometimes have trouble raising heat-loving vegetables such as yellow crook-neck summer squash. So one year we decided to try sheets of black plastic over the beds. First we stretched the plastic out over the prepared and soaked beds, anchoring it firmly all around with soil shoveled up over the edges. Then we made ten-inch slits in the plastic with a single edge razor wherever we intended to have our plants, and set in the seedlings (which already had the second or true leaves) through the slits. It was necessary to heap soil on *top* of the plastic in at least an eight-inch circle around the little seedling. If we didn't, the wind tended to get in under the plastic through the slits, whipping the sheets right off the beds, beheading the plants. Furthermore, the heat was so great on the south side of the seedling that it tended to fry the young plants while the roots were still small and near the surface.

By comparison with beds not covered in this way, we did have very high yields on both winter and summer squashes. This must have been due to the much higher soil temperatures under the black plastic. We found that months, rather than weeks, could go by between waterings. When it was necessary to soak the ground again, we slipped a hose in through the slits and allowed it to run slowly for half an hour or so around the base of each plant. The position of the hose end has to be moved now and then. Water does not tend to spread out sideways the way it soaks down directly into the ground.

But we have a problem about using plastic. Not only is it made from nonrenewable fossil materials which are becoming scarce, but when it gets old and full of holes and tears, it creates a waste-management problem since it can't be broken down by microorganisms. So, in spite of the good effect it had on the raised soil temperatures, once those original sheets of plastic wore out, which they did in one season, we never used any again.

Compost is a superior mulch for container-grown plants. If the surface is kept evenly moist it is less likely to shrink away from the sides of the box or can. For rooftops, where wind is a problem, cutting out a piece of burlap the shape of the top of the container and fitting it around the stem of the plant over the top of the mulch helps to keep the compost from drying out and blowing away. You can tuck the edges down into the soil around the inside edge of the container and put a few big stones on top to make sure.

Besides being lost from the open ground by evaporation, water is also lost by plants. The leaves of seed plants have many small openings, called stomata, surrounded by two guard cells. The whole structure looks rather like a doughnut or an inner tube under the microscope. When there is plenty of water available to the plant, the plant tissues, and thus the guard cells, are plump and the hole is open. When these guard cells lose their plumpness they collapse, closing the hole and reducing water loss. However, this is really an imperfect process. In the heat of the day during midsummer, it is common to see the large leaves of squash plants wilting slightly in the sun. Watering will do no good, for the leaves are simply losing water faster than the roots can take it in. They will usually completely recover as shade or the cooler air reaches them.

There may be a problem with water loss in transplanting young seedlings. Water is absorbed by plants mostly through the small, fuzzy, white, one-cell-large root hairs which form right behind the growing tip of the root. As they are very fragile, the movement of the little seedlings from the container where they were started to the ground outdoors very often damages these root hairs, thus crippling the plant's ability to take in water. The mechanism for preventing water loss being as imperfect as it is, the seedling may become irretrievably wilted before enough new root hairs have had the time to grow and the plant can start absorbing water again.

This is one of the several reasons that, were you to look at our garden during the dry warm part of the year, you would see a little forest of overturned earthen flower pots. They make perfect protection to the newly set out seedlings. Since increased temperature and wind velocity also influences the rate at which plants transpire water, covering them for the first day or two after transplanting with an overturned flower pot solves both conditions. The seedlings are shaded, and the wind is prevented from blowing away the wet saturated air immediately around them.

Rules on Watering

1. Water thoroughly but infrequently. The top eight to ten inches should be wet. To decide how often and how long to water, you need to know the texture of your soil (heavy or light) and how much water your sprinkler delivers in an hour. Then adjust the time to fit how windy and warm it was in the period since you last watered. The hotter and windier, the sooner you need to water again.

2. Water in the cool part of the day when not too windy, to avoid unnecessary evaporation.

3. Water early in the day to allow the plants to dry off. This will help discourage the growth of disease. Contrary to myth, a drop of water on the leaf does not operate like a magnifier and produce spots.

4. Cover seedlings with overturned pots or other protection during the first day or two after transplanting.

5. Use mulches whenever possible.

6. Check the depth of soil moisture in your garden with a spade.

Now, to get off a little steam, we must say something about a dreadful practice that is very common in urban areas: standing about with a hose, sprinkling by hand. To be sure, this is usually done on front lawns and for the purpose of giving the person a chance to get outdoors and see what's happening in the neighborhood, but even if it has social justifications, it is a very poor watering practice. Too little water is delivered this way, as few people have the patience to stand in one spot for the time it takes to soak the lawn thoroughly; thus only the top inches get wet. This encourages the grass roots to grow up in the top layer of soil where they are more subject to damage from sunburn, traffic, and disease. It may encourage tree roots to become surface feeders, causing all kinds of problems as they pop up sidewalks. It is best to soak deeply, an hour or so in each spot depending upon your type of soil, and then let the surface dry out between waterings. This will encourage the roots to seek water at greater depths.

There are some special circumstances which demand exceptions from the rules just mentioned. Seedbeds must be kept moist. If they are outdoors in hot weather this may mean a watering several times a day, as seeds must not dry out during germination. Certain mature plants that originate in foggy areas enjoy a daily misting, for instance, some ferns, mosses, rhododendrons, azaleas, and fuschias. On the other hand, some plants, such as cactus, will only blossom and do their best if left entirely dry for a period of several months each year.

Containers need special watering too. More about that

when we discuss container and rooftop gardening in detail (Chapter 11).

One last comment about watering. Furrow irrigation, where you dig little ditches and plant on each side as is done in irrigated agriculture, uses more water than overhead sprinkling, but is superior for some plants that are susceptible to mildew in cool climates, for example, squashes and peas. Overhead watering can also reduce some insect problems directly by washing the insects off, and indirectly by creating the proper moisture conditions for diseases.

Water carefully and not wastefully—for water is precious, purchased with energy, and if too much is used, it will wash nutrients down below the reach of plant roots.

Structure

There's a saying among soil scientists, "You can't do anything about soil texture, but you can improve soil structure." When we heard that the first time, two questions came to mind. First of all, what is soil "structure," compared to texture, and secondly, is the saying true for the city gardener as well as the farmer?

The structure of a soil is the way in which the sand, silt, and clay particles are arranged. Ideally the particles are not all the same distance from each other. Rather, they are clumped together in combinations of groups of grains, or aggregates, with spaces between the clumps. This granulation of the soil is promoted by a number of things. For instance: 1. freezing and thawing; 2. expansion and contraction of water films around the soil particles; 3. action of plant roots growing and dying; 4. presence of a network of fungal mycelium (those thin, white, intertwining threads that are the fungus plants) in the top eight inches or so of the soil; and 5. mixing effects of the soil animals.

The animals and plants secrete complex sugars (organic gums and polysaccharides), and these coat the soil particles with a slime which helps the aggregates to stay together. Unless the soil granules are stabilized by coatings of organic matter or their own electrochemical properties, they will gradually coalesce into larger and larger clods.

Have you ever seen a mature tree growing from a crack in a huge rock? Maybe you thought it was the tree root that started the crack in the first place. Not so. There has to be a space there already in which the tree root can get started. Once established, by slowly adding to its width, a plant can actually force the two halves of the rock apart along the crack. But the tiny fragile tip of a plant root can only grow longer if it can find a space to grow into.

This is one reason a compacted soil, or a compacted layer of hard pan in your soil, can limit the growth of plants. Roots cannot penetrate where there are not already spaces to grow into. Thus, well-structured (that is, well-aggregated) soils with lots of spaces for plant roots are important in growing plants. Structure refers to the kind of characteristic sizes of spaces or pores in the soil.

Believe it or not, a soil with a good structure will be 50 percent empty space. When Helga was in college, being an admirer of Chinese culture, she read a lot of ancient Chinese poetry and philosophy. She remembers being impressed by a Taoist text which pointed out that it was precisely the empty or "nothing" part of a cup that made the cup useful. For if it was solid, it could not be used to contain something. So it is with a good soil. The empty spaces in the soil are just as important as the soil particles, for it is in these pores that water and air are held, and plant roots and soil organisms need both.

Now, it is true that some plant roots can stand conditions with less air than others, those that grow in marshes, for instance. Cranberries, rice, celery, even broccoli and cauliflower, are plants that can stand various degrees of waterlogged soils for periods of time. On the other hand, some plants—common fruit trees are a good example—may be very sensitive to poor drainage. (See Chapter 8, on planting fruit trees.)

When airless, or anaerobic conditions exist in the soil, different bacteria start to grow and toxic materials may be formed, hydrogen sulfide, for instance. Since carbon dioxide is breathed out, or respired, by both living plant roots and soil animals, this can also collect around the roots and exclude oxygen. At high levels it is also toxic to plants. So, good soil structure, with plenty of spaces for the free exchange of gasses with the air, is important.

The total amount of pore space is less important than the characteristic sizes of the spaces. From this point of view, a clay soil may have more pore space but be less suitable for plants than a sandy one. This is because the sizes of the clay particles are so small that the spaces between them are small too. Thus air and water move through very slowly. It is rather like the difference in air spaces that you get when you pack sesame seeds, compared to walnuts, in a jar. The bigger the objects, the bigger the spaces in between. Remember too that some clay particles have the ability to absorb water between their sandwich layers, causing them to swell and thus to further block the passage of water, air, or plant roots.

Actually, a good soil will have large and small spaces, all held open because the soil aggregates or clumps are coated with organic slime, as mentioned before. When you water, the large pore spaces will fill and then drain by gravity, fairly rapidly. Oxygen will enter the soil where the pores have drained. The small pore spaces will absorb and retain water by capillary action.

A good soil texture can be destroyed in a number of ways. The most common method in urban areas is by compaction through walking or driving on the soil. Never walk on the beds or soil where you will grow plants.

Continuous cropping without returning enough organic matter to the soil will also gradually destroy porosity. This is seen where corn, a plant that produces very little easily decomposed root material, is grown year after year in the same place. Gradually the soil structure becomes poorer and poorer, since there is little organic matter to feed soil organisms that maintain the soil aggregates.

Tilling, or cultivating, the soil will also destroy soil aggregates. In the short run it may leave the soil looser, especially if it is used to incorporate organic material. However, over the long term it may have undesirable effects, by breaking the stable soil aggregates as well as through hastening the oxidation of organic matter by exposing it to air and sun. The worst offenders are roto-tillers. They may appear to leave the soil fluffy, but after a couple of waterings it will be more compacted than before. The blades, in churning, actually smash the soil particles together. Your only excuse for using a roto-tiller in an urban garden is if you have a huge compacted area to cover and wish to dig in a great deal of well-composted organic matter the first time.

It is best to use a digging fork, if you feel you must turn the soil. When you do so, mix your compost lightly into the *top few inches* of the beds. Organic matter buried deeply will not have enough oxygen to enable soil micro- and macro-organisms to decompose it satisfactorily.

The easiest way to destroy the structure of the soil that has fair amounts of clay is to disturb it when it is wet. This will cause the aggregates to collapse and is called "puddling." The result of turning a clay soil when it is wet: big, heavy, hard-to-break-up clumps of earth when it is dry. How to tell when a clay soil can be disturbed? When it has drained sufficiently so there is no longer any shine when you slice into it with a spade.

What to do if your soil has lots of clay in it and the spring is so wet that it never does seem to dry out enough to plant? Here's what we do in our backyard, where we have a heavy clay adobe, yet the rainy winter and spring weather are so mild that we can grow plants around the year. First, we raise the level of our beds six to eight inches higher than the pathways between them. We did this originally by digging out the walks as shallow trenches and throwing the soil onto the areas that were to become beds. In some areas we held the sides up with boards. Then we heaped four to six inches of compost on top; this we renew as fast as we can produce it.

This has had two wonderful results. Even during the heaviest rains we can still plant out the seedlings that we start inside on the window sill. We simply part the mulch, set the seedling in, and tuck the mulch back *firmly* around it. That way we do not disturb the soil itself at all. In addition, this organic matter is placed just where there is the most oxygen available for the microorganisms and soil animals to decompose it. The nutrients thus released are watered down to the area of the plant roots. After four consecutive years of this treatment, the top layers of our hard adobe had become so soft and friable that one can plunge one's hand right in up to the knuckles, even the wrist in some areas. Through the action of the larger animals, such as earthworms, this improvement of the soil is

trenches and beds without support from boards
(cut-away view)

bed sides up with boards
(cut-away view)

continuing, deeper and deeper every year as more pore space and thus more oxygen becomes available to organisms penetrating further into the ground. We tell people, "Forget turning the soil—let the worms do it for you."

How to Improve the Structure of Your Soil

1. Add organic matter—well-made compost is the best. In clay soil, this will increase aggregation and pore space. In sandy soils it will increase water and nutrient-holding capacities. In all soils it will provide nutrient materials for varied soil fauna, the activities of which aid in forming soil aggregates.

2. Till the soil as little as possible—once a year or not at all—only to add organic matter, if necessary. Tillage is usually done to remove weeds, but weeding is better handled by mulching, because mulches smother weed seedlings, make large weeds easier to pull by keeping the ground surface soft and moist, improve water penetration when it rains or when you irrigate, reduce erosion of the soil surface, eliminate rain compaction and mud splattering (the latter is sometimes important in transmission of plant

disease), and finally, they add organic matter to the area where most of the microorganisms are that can decompose it.

3. Rotate your crops. Alternate with legumes (peas and beans), whenever possible.

Not infrequently, at this point in a discussion of how to manage the soil, someone will wail, "I've just rented a house with a neglected backyard big enough to grow a little food. But the soil is impossible. It's heavy clay, all covered with weeds—I've got to turn it." Here is our suggestion on what to do. Cut down the weeds, cover the ground with a heavy (one foot, if possible) layer of compost or other mulch such as decomposed manure and straw from a stable, or piles of leaves. Let the rains, regular weekly watering, or snow start decomposition. Let it be for a while. After a month or so (just time to get all settled in your new house) depending on the weather—the warmer it is the faster the material will decompose—mix the partially decomposed materials lightly into the top few inches of the soil. Add a little nitrogen; this can be blood meal, human urine, high nitrogen manure, or compost, and you are ready to go. Just prepare and plant one area at a time. "Start small" is a good motto for urban gardeners.

Now that you know what soil structure is, how about the answer to the other question we started with? Can you change the texture of the soil? Well, a farmer can't, because he has too much area to deal with. Even increasing the proportion of sand from 10 to 30 percent in a clay carrot bed two feet wide, ten feet long, and one foot deep takes an awful lot of sand—about five cubic feet. (Furthermore, as time goes on, the sand may migrate downward through the clay.) If you are investing in several cubic yards of good "loam" for your yard, be sure to mix the lower portion of it with the less fertile subsoil beneath it. Too abrupt a transition will create drainage problems (much as a pan would).

Where you *can* greatly influence the texture of a soil is in container gardening. There you can have just the mixture of sand and clay you choose. More about that later.

chapter 5

Why Compost?

All the energy that some folks put into fertilizing and weeding, we put into composting. With our methods of making and using compost, those other jobs almost take care of themselves. We've written so much about compost already, you must think we regard it as the cure-all for everything from weak eyesight to Aunt Mary's lumbago!

Why should you compost? It's an ideal way of handling the organic wastes that accumulate around an ordinary household—kitchen garbage, weeds, grass clippings, ashes, bits of paper, dust from the vacuum cleaner, etc. Since all of these materials originated from growing plants, they all contain the nutrients that plants need to grow. What could be better than recycling them back into plant life again?

What happens in a compost? Bacteria, fungi, and other organisms break down complex organic materials into the simpler compounds that plants can absorb through their plant roots. This process may be aerobic, in the presence of oxygen, or anaerobic, without oxygen, as beneath the waters of a swamp or in the tank of a methane generator. Different organisms are involved in these two processes and different by-products are the result.

The method that we use and recommend for the urban gardener is a "fast" aerobic process. If managed properly there will be no offending smells to alarm the neighbors. In fact, smell is one of the ways you can monitor the pile— bad smells mean not enough air is getting to the contents of the pile and you will want to remedy that in one of the ways we will suggest.

The finished product is useful as a mulch (we layer it three to four inches thick)—to conserve moisture, modify the surface temperature changes of the soil, protect the soil from erosion by water and compaction by foot traffic, and provide habitat and food for numerous soil organisms. Compost is the ideal form in which to incorporate organic materials into the soil, for the materials have been digested by the organisms in the pile to the point where further decomposition will not deplete soil nitrogen. As we have pointed out before, organic material in the soil is essential to the development of soil aggregates and pore space for oxygen and other gas exchanges necessary for plant roots, as well as increased water and plant nutrient retention.

If you follow our directions very carefully, you will have a compost that is more than just a good soil amendment useful for improving soil structure. It can actually function as a fertilizer, providing nitrogen and the other nutrients needed for plant growth. Remember, nitrogen is frequently the plant nutrient in shortest supply since it is used in large amounts by plants, is easily leached from the soil by water, and is replenished very slowly by the soil organisms under most natural conditions. To make a good compost that is high in nitrogen is somewhat like making a fine stew—it is a mixture of science and art!

Methods, Slow and Fast

If you should mention the word "compost" in a group of devoted organic gardeners, as we did at a garden club talk recently, you may suddenly find yourself in the midst of a hearty brawl. Everyone will want to tell you how he does it, what his authority says about it, and what's wrong with the other fellow's way. For some of us, composting is pursued with a religious fervor. We can get the attention of our students by talking about a "compost yoga," referring to "compost gurus," and exhorting those who have a taboo regarding waste products to rise to "turd consciousness." We have become compost fanatics!

However, underneath all the claims and counter-claims regarding superior methods, you will find that there are basically two main styles: slow and fast.

The slow methods have a great deal of appeal. They are very simple to follow and do not take much time or physical energy. Most of the slow methods are variations on the following: leaves, grass clippings, and weeds are heaped in a pile, with or without occasional sprinklings of soil, and these are left to decompose by themselves. There are so many good descriptions available of these methods that we will not repeat them in detail here. These piles may heat up, particularly in the center of the heap, but most of the decomposition will be provided by fungi which thrive under cooler conditions and can survive with less oxygen and handle a more acid environment than many of the decomposer bacteria.

The slower methods proceed well in cool, moist weather. They are popular in England and wherever summer rains are frequent enough to keep the pile moist. If a windrow, or row of little piles, is begun in the early spring and completed by the late fall when the snows melt again, the material will be ready to use. The advantage, besides simplicity, is that one does not have to worry about a nitrogen source for the organisms in the pile. They will work very slowly, with whatever nitrogen is available.

The disadvantages of this easy method are that the resulting pile will be low in nitrogen, the piles take up considerable room, and the temperature rarely rises high enough throughout the *whole* pile to kill the pathogens, or disease-causing organisms, that cause plant disease. Furthermore, it is definitely not advisable for the city farmer to use a slow pile to recycle his kitchen garbage because this will cause fly breeding and rodent problems. Even slow piles that contain no garbage but have too high a percentage of grass clippings or become too moist may

encourage fly production without the compost maker realizing it. So, while many excellent slow-composting methods, in pits, in piles covered with sod, or in open bins, are
fine for the suburban family with a large lot or the rural
household, they are just not suitable for the city farm. On
a small lot where space is at a premium and neighbors
become quickly annoyed by smells or flies, it is best to
turn to a method that minimizes these problems.

The Way We Do It

There are a number of styles of fast composting. They all
take more attention, energy, and thought than the slow
methods. We are going to describe the one we use and
recommend to our students and other urban farmers. If
you follow our directions carefully and take the time to
understand the theory behind the techniques, you can
learn to produce a high nitrogen compost out of materials
generally regarded as waste products and a nuisance. The
finished product will be available quickly, in approximately three weeks, and will provide a complete plant fertilizer
as well as act as a soil amendment and be useful as a
mulch. You will be able to keep fly and rodent problems
to a minimum.

Furthermore, all the materials in the pile will be subjected to temperatures high enough to kill most plant pathogens and even take apart most pesticides (except the chlorinated hydrocarbons related to DDT). This means you
will be able to use the pile to dispose of diseased plant
material as well as to recycle all your organic garbage. If
you take the trouble to build attractive bins, your composting area should appear sufficiently neat so as not to
antagonize neighbors or your local public health authorities.

Choosing a Location and Making Bins

If possible, select a shady place so that the piles will not dry out too quickly. The north side of a garage, the house, or some shrubbery is often perfect. Ideally, you should have a spot three or four feet wide and from nine to twelve feet long. Such spaces are often found as wasted areas between two houses, where it is so shady that nothing will grow but there is not enough width to do anything else there either. The best possible situation is where you

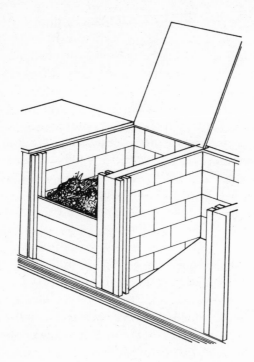

compost bins with cinder block sides, plywood lids, and slatted fronts

can construct three bins, each one of them approximately a cubic yard in size.

The front of the bins should be made of removable boards, allowing easy entry as the contents are emptied. The sides and floor of the bins should be as tight as possible so that bits of organic matter cannot fall through and provide overlooked fly-breeding material underneath and outside of the bins. The lids should be tight enough to keep out the rain. Some people construct their bins right on the earth without a wooden or concrete floor. However, this allows nutrient-filled juices to run off and be lost from the pile. We prefer to capture any run-off with a layer of sawdust at the bottom of the bin which is then turned with the rest of the pile. Our own bins are made of cinder block, with a concrete floor and painted exterior plywood tops. In the student garden we have built them of scrap and regular lumber and these have been perfectly satisfactory as long as there were no cracks between the boards. If you are using irregular salvaged lumber, you can caulk the cracks with wood putty when the bins are built.

Students of ours have made compost in large, twenty-gallon plastic garbage cans, and even small, five-gallon cans. The difficulty with using such small containers is that the pile is not large enough to hold the necessary heat and it takes longer to process completely. Starting out with about a cubic yard of material seems to give the best results. As the pile decomposes, this amount will shrink quite a bit, depending on the actual contents.

Usually it takes us about a week or so to use up the compost once it is made, as we don't have much time to devote to gardening generally. Since it takes about three weeks for a batch to be ready for use, this means we end up making one every month or so. However, there are times during the summer when both our garden needs and garden wastes demand a more rigorous attention to the system. Then, with the three-bin system, it is possible to make a compost every two weeks. That way there is one batch cooking and one being used up all the time. If that sounds like too much work, then settle for the two-bin system, but you will need at least two, since you will need to turn the materials back and forth between the bins to mix and aerate them thoroughly.

Collecting the Materials

There are two parts to the question of what to use in the compost. The first is where to find it and the second is where to store it. Sometimes the latter is the biggest problem.

When Bill worked in the state public health department, he learned that they had done a study on the garbage cans in our area and came to the conclusion that the average can produced, in warm weather, about a thousand flies a week! Very few householders are aware of that. The fact is that flies are attracted to smells, can slip through an eighth of an inch space, and in warm weather a new generation may be produced in just six or seven days.

Since one of the important ingredients of the compost is your kitchen wastes—onion skins, banana peels, orange rinds, egg shells, spoiled food, and scraps from the table that don't go to the pets, etc.—and since, if you are only making a compost once every four weeks or so, you have to store these materials for a while, it becomes necessary to find a way to do this without producing flies. Here is a method which has proved foolproof.

1. Obtain a number of five-gallon cans. We have about eight of the plastic ones with lids and metal snap-over handles, so they are reasonably easy to move around (plastic makes no noise and does not rust).

2. Find a good source of fine grain sawdust. There is a

cabinet shop not far from us that disposes of tons of it near their rear exit. If sawdust is unavailable, use ashes, soil, or dry leaves.

3. Provide a storage area for this sawdust close to where you take out your kitchen refuse. We keep ours in a plastic barrel right on our back porch, with a smaller can inside with which to dip out the sawdust.

4. Each time you bring out the kitchen garbage and put it into a five-gallon can, cover the material with at least an inch of sawdust. Make sure that everything is well covered and that no kitchen wastes are left exposed. If there is no smell coming from the can, the flies will not be attracted to lay eggs in it. We gave this method the ultimate test on the Antioch College West farm this last summer. A chicken had died, so we buried it in a five-gallon can of sawdust (mainly softwood) and left it for about three months during the summer. Temperatures in the California interior valleys where this farm is located often reach 100° F during midday. At the end of the summer, we uncovered the chicken, planning to put it into the center of a hot com-

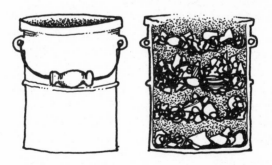

5 gal. plastic cans for compost...
sand and garbage layers

post pile. It did not smell at all and had barely begun to visibly decompose!

5. When you get to the top of the can, finish with a layer of sawdust. Then set the can aside to wait for when you build the next compost, and start on another can.

What else besides kitchen garbage might go into the compost? All organic materials can be decomposed by microorganisms, but some break down much more quickly than others. Fats go very slowly and should be kept out of slow compost piles. However, in the method we are advocating they can be handled just fine. Nevertheless, we recommend leaving fats and meat scraps out of your piles until you are sure of the technique. Many plant resins are resistant. Eucalyptus leaves, conifer needles, and similar plant materials should probably be left to decompose slowly under the trees where they drop, rather than put in the compost pile. You may need to do a little experimenting to learn which of the organic materials available to you in your area are too difficult to compost by the following method. Still, nearly everything once alive can be handled if added in small amounts.

Grass clippings are wonderful for the compost, but we don't have any lawn. Luckily, urban areas are filled with people who spend vast amounts of money to grade, plant, fertilize, water, and mow their lawn and then throw the harvest out. So, if you ask around among your neighbors, gardeners for school grounds, or city parks maintenance people, you should be able to locate a source of clippings. (A hired gardener of a neighbor down the street leaves a little pile of grass cuttings at our garage door on a regular basis.) When you are considering sources for grass clippings, keep in mind that there may be undesirable lead accumulations in lawns along busy streets and avoid those. The same advice applies to leaves for your compost. We

you will be able to smell the ammonia gas coming off the pile.

Kitchen garbage is usually very high in nitrogen, as are grass clippings. If the pile will contain a very high proportion of such materials then little or no additional sources of nitrogen may be needed. A student of ours very successfully composted the daily kitchen garbage of an entire student housing unit by just mixing these wastes with sawdust and proceeding as we will describe here.

In most compost piles, however, it is desirable to add some nitrogen. Some manures, such as chicken, rabbit, *fresh* steer and dog manure, are high in this plant nutrient. So is human urine which we recommend for this purpose. Blood meal, hoof and horn meal are good but expensive sources. The microorganisms will work happily with the cheapest source of nitrogen with which you can supply them. One of the easiest and least expensive to obtain is ammonium sulphate.

The problem with these synthesized fertilizers is that it takes fossil fuel energy to produce them. If used directly in the soil without the addition of compost as they sometimes are in commercial agriculture, they are inadequate because they do not return organic material to the earth. As you realize by now, organic material incorporated in the soil has many crucial functions besides just supplying plant nutrients. However, in the compost pile such a synthetic fertilizer is acceptable if none other is available. The microbes do not seem to distinguish between the synthesized and naturally occurring forms of nitrogen, and the finished compost will be satisfactory.

We recommend building the pile in layers. Of course, the first time you turn it, all the materials will get mixed up, but layering does help you in starting the pile to keep track of how much of each material you are adding. Estimate the proportion of carbon to nitrogen the best you can. Some corrections can be made during the first and second turnings, based on how you judge the process to be proceeding.

Building the Pile

When you have all your materials accumulated, it's time to build the pile.

Start with some absorbent material on the bottom of the bin. We like to use sawdust for this. (As you have discovered by now, sawdust is one of the important raw materials we use to run our urban farm: to store kitchen garbage, to collect manure under our chickens and rabbits, in pathways between the beds of plants to discourage weeds and snails and prevent compaction, and to add carbon and absorb juices in the compost pile.)

After the sawdust you can start making alternate layers of green and dry matter, and manure if you are using it. If some other nitrogen source is used, sprinkle it over the layers as you go along. (If you are using urine, do *not* dilute it with water.) Make a three- to five-inch layer of each of your materials until the bin is full.

The smaller the size of the materials you put in, the more surface area you expose to decomposition, the faster the pile will go. For this reason you may wish to chop up the coarse materials—melon rinds, dry weed stalks, or straw, etc.—into shorter lengths (three to eight inches) with a cleaver. When we first began composting, impressed by the ads in garden magazines, we decided to get ourselves a grinder-shredder. We shopped around and finally invested in a medium-priced one ($160), and used it faithfully for many months. It made a great deal of noise, so we used earplugs, and it would frequently get jammed, and we'd have to stop and fuss with it. It also consumed fossil fuel and needed careful use to prevent losing fingers. We were beginning to have second thoughts about American food-producing methods and the amount of fossil fuel energy used, compared to the amount of energy in food calories produced.

We stopped using the compost grinder and haven't used it since. We found it was totally unnecessary. Since then we have made many composts successfully with a cleaver and some without.

No commercially sold materials need be added to the pile. We particularly advise against the addition of lime to the pile. Lime in the pile will promote the loss of nitrogen which will volatilize as ammonia. If your soil is too acid, if you are fertilizing regularly with an acid fertilizer such as human urine, add lime to the soil itself. If you are in an area with soils that are extremely phosphorus-deficient and are planning to use rock phosphate or bone meal as a source of this mineral, then you may want to add these to the pile to start their decomposition. But this will be a great waste of money if you don't need phosphorus, so don't just add it automatically because you read it in a book somewhere. If you have a mixture of vegetable refuse, grass, weeds, and leaves in the pile, you should have *all* the phosphorus you need without buying rock or other powdered materials. Commercially sold compost starters have not been shown to make any difference in small piles. The spores of the organisms that decompose organic material are everywhere and need only the proper environment to germinate and begin work.

When you have finished building the pile, you should have about a cubic yard of material. A smaller pile does not hold the heat adequately, and a larger one takes longer to turn.

After the pile is built, you may need to water it. If you have been adding urine every other layer or so, it may be wet enough. It should be moist, but not too wet, as there needs to be plenty of air throughout the pile. *No water should be running out at the bottom.* If this should happen at any time, put a thick layer of sawdust or dry leaves into the adjoining bin and turn the pile over into that one to trap the juices that otherwise would produce flies or be lost.

Turning the Pile

After the pile is built, let it rest for a day or so. Then, with a pitchfork, turn the compost into the neighboring bin, examining it while you do so. The top, bottom, and sides of the old pile should be turned into the center of the new bin, the center of the old pile around the edges of the new. This should be done each time the pile is turned to ensure that all materials are exposed to the heat of the center, killing any fly eggs, larvae, and plant pathogens.

The turning also introduces air into the pile, which is essential for the growth of the desirable microbes. If this is not done, the bacteria will exhaust their oxygen and then a different group of organisms (anaerobic), that can live in this new environment, will start to grow and multiply. These anaerobic bacteria will not heat the pile as hot and can produce highly objectionable odors. Knowing this, various people have designed bins or other containers with openings in the sides to permit better aeration. We advise against this, because it will increase heat loss and there will be fly breeding around the edges where it is cool.

The pile should be mixed and turned in this fashion at least every third day. Turning it more often (up to once a day) will speed the process of decomposition. If the pile is properly made, for the first few days the temperature in the center of the pile will rise, reading approximately 160° F by the third or fourth day. It will return to this temperature each time the pile is turned for many days and then begin to cool slowly. When it has cooled down completely, it is finished. However, it can be put out in the garden as soon as the temperature has gone below 100°F.

Reading about composting is rather like reading about cooking. There is no substitute for actually making one or two piles and learning the proper proportion of ingredients by experience. If you find that the smell of ammonia is noticeable, that means that you have too much nitrogen in the pile and the bacteria are respiring off the extra. Flies attracted to the pile are also an indication that ammonia is being lost. You don't want to lose this valuable plant nutrient, so the best thing is to trap it by adding some more carbon (sawdust or leaves) to the pile to get a better ratio of the two. If the ammonia smell persists after the pile has cooled down and appears otherwise ready to use, do not place the compost close to growing plants (within four or five inches of the stems), as you risk causing nitrogen burn. This can happen with compost just as it can when you use "hot" or "fresh" (high in nitrogen) manures or the synthetic fertilizers. Chicken manure is so "hot" that it should never be used directly on the soil, but always put through the compost. Incidentally, fine composts for raising mushrooms have been made using just chicken manure and sawdusts.

If the pile cools down but still contains some chunks of materials that appear to you not to be decomposed enough from their original condition, sift the compost through a coarse screen. The undecomposed pieces can go back into the next compost to go through the process again.

We don't usually turn the compost into the soil nowadays, although we did so the first year we grew vegetables in the backyard. Now we just let the earthworms and other soil animals do the turning for us. The soil, which is a heavy clay, has become loose and porous.

If you do decide to turn the soil, use a digging fork, never a roto-tiller, as the latter will destroy those very soil aggregates you are working hard to develop. The soil may seem fluffier right after you finish using a roto-tiller, but controlled tests have shown that after it rains, or you irrigate, the soil will be more compacted than before you used the machine. Think about it too: the roto-tiller blades as they cut through the soil actually shear a layer of soil off every turn. This shearing action smashes the clay particles together, producing a more compacted soil.

To summarize the entire process:

1. Select and prepare the composting area.

2. Assemble your materials.

3. Chop as fine as possible, filling the bin with alternate layers of green matter, dry or high-carbon materials, and a source of nitrogen.

4. At intervals while building the pile, or when finished, add a sprinkling of water.

5. Turn the compost every second or third day into the neighboring bin, using a pitchfork. In turning, mix the materials thoroughly—former top goes to bottom, outside matter into the center. Avoid spilling material outside the bins: it may be a source of fly breeding.

6. While turning, examine the pile for fly larvae. Center heat will kill them.

7. Notice differences between piles as to age, particle size, moisture, odors. Does the pile smell like ammonia? Is it almost too hot to touch in the center? Is it moist?

8. Finish turning the pile with a flat shovel, and broom if necessary. The bin should be clean when it is empty, or before introducing the next pile.

If compost does not heat up high (160°F) within two days, the possibilities are these: a) not enough nitrogen (add some blood meal, urine, etc.); b) too dry (add water while turning); c) too much water (add a little sawdust or dry leaves while turning); or d) not enough oxygen (turn more frequently).

If the pile is giving off a strong ammonia smell, there is too much material high in nitrogen (add a sprinkling of sawdust while turning).

Using Compost

Compost may be used on top of beds around plants as a mulch.

Finished compost may be spread out on newly harvested beds and turned in before replanting.

Finished compost may be sifted. Sifted compost can be used in seed beds or flats. In carrot beds, for instance, a good mixture is one-third each of sand, sifted dirt, and sifted compost. Coarse particles should be returned to a new compost pile to break down further.

Unfinished (still hot) compost may be spaded into the ground *only* if it has had at least a week of composting and if no planting in that spot is to follow immediately. The further decomposition of the material in the soil by bacteria requires nitrogen, just as it does in the bin. Thus, raw compost may cause a temporary deficiency of nitrogen in the soil if it is low in this nutrient. If the compost contains much manure that has not broken down sufficiently, or if there is a strong ammonia smell coming from it, this may cause damage to the plants from excessive nitrogen.

Caution: If the ammonia smell persists heavily after the compost has cooled, do not use it close to plants (within four or five inches of stems) as you risk causing nitrogen burn. Next time use proportionately less manure or more vegetable matter when making your compost pile.

chapter 6

What Do Plants Need?

See Hopk n's Cafe!

Sooner or later a student of plant nutrition may be told, "See Hopk n's Cafe, mighty good club, Cousin Moman." (Or written out, C'HOPK N'S Cafe MgClB, CuZnMoMn). This is a handy way of remembering which minerals are needed for plant growth. The words stand for the chemical symbols: C(carbon), H(hydrogen), O(oxygen), P(phosphorus), K(potassium), N(nitrogen), S(sulphur), Ca(calcium), Fe(iron), Mg(magnesium), Cl(chlorine), B(boron), Cu(copper), Zn(zinc), Mo(molybdenum), and Mn(manganese). Recent research indicates that sodium (Na) should also be included.

Most of these minerals reach the plant only through its roots, while carbon, hydrogen, oxygen, and some nitrogen are available from the air. Phosphorus, potassium, nitrogen, and sulfur are referred to as macronutrients. This means they are used in large quantities. For instance, nitrogen is needed in amounts of approximately 100 to 300 pounds per acre, phosphorus at approximately 300 pounds per acre, and potassium at about 100 to 200 pounds per acre. By comparison, calcium might be used at the rate of fifty pounds per acre. Magnesium, chlorine, and boron are regarded as micronutrients for they are required in much smaller quantities. The final minerals in the list above, copper, zinc, molybdenum, and manganese, are needed in still smaller, sometimes only trace, amounts. Compare the use of zinc at six to twelve pounds per acre and molybdenum at one-half pound per acre with the demand for the macronutrients, or NPKS as they are referred to.

These minerals are available to plants as very small particles, atoms or groups of atoms which bear electrical charges. Do you remember when we described in Chapter 4 the small, flat platelets that make up clays? These clay surfaces carry negative charges, as do organic materials such as compost or humus, and therein lies their great value in soils. Since a number of the most important minerals needed for plant growth are positively charged, they are attracted to the negative charges on the clays and pieces of organic matter and are thus temporarily held in the soil available to plant roots. You can visualize this by remembering the way the positive and negative poles of two magnets will attract each other.

Sands and silts do not have this ability to hold on to and exchange plant nutrients. It is said they have a low exchange capacity. Organic matter has an even higher exchange capacity than clay. So now, perhaps, you can begin to appreciate another way the incorporation of organic matter into the soil by earthworms and other soil animals, and its gradual decomposition into smaller and smaller particles by microorganisms, is so important.

Potassium, calcium, ammonium (a form of nitrogen present in the soil in only small amounts), magnesium, and sodium are all usually present in the soil as positively charged particles and are sometimes referred to as bases. On the other hand, the common forms in which nitrogen and phosphorus are found in the soil, nitrate and phosphate, as well as chemical compounds of carbon, sulfur, and chlorine, are all negatively charged as are the clay particles. Since two negatively charged particles will repel each other, these valuable plant nutrients may not be held long in the soil, but rather are easily leached away with every rain or irrigation. Nitrogen compounds are even more soluble in water than those with phosphorus. Since nitrogen, phosphorus, and sulfur are all needed by growing plants in fairly substantial amounts, the urban gardener must see to it that these are replenished regularly.

The Mysteries of pH or
Soil Acidity

There is another part to this story: a water molecule (H_2O) is composed of two atoms of hydrogen and one of oxygen. In the soil this molecule often splits into two parts, an atom of hydrogen, which is small and positively charged, and an O-H part, which is called the hydroxyl ion and is negative. The relative proportions of these two in the soil determines whether the soil is "acid" (more hydrogen ions), "alkaline" (more hydroxyl ions), or "neutral" (the same of both)—sometimes referred to as "sweet."

The free, small hydrogen ion is able to slip in close to the clay surface, knocking off the other minerals, or bases, such as calcium and magnesium. Thus in areas with high rainfall, the soils may slowly become acidic as other minerals are replaced by hydrogen ions from the rain water. Where little water is available to wash them away, clay surfaces may be covered with calcium, magnesium, and sodium ions, thus creating the alkaline soils of arid regions.

A logarithmic scale has been developed to measure this range of acid to alkaline conditions. It is called the pH scale or Power of Hydrogen. A pH of 7 is neutral, below that is acid (pH 1 to 6), and above, alkaline (pH 8 to 14). Lemon juice has a pH of 3. Some commercial soft drinks are even more acid, which is one good reason to discourage their consumption by children. The acid eats into the soft enamel of young teeth, and the sugar in the drink feeds the bacteria of decay that live in the mouth.

Orange juice has a pH of about 4. Acid-loving plants such as blueberries, cranberries, azaleas, camellias, hydrangeas, gardenias, and rhododendrons grow well around pH 5. Potatoes and sweet potatoes do well around a pH of 5.5, which is still acid enough to discourage scab, a disease of potatoes which may flourish in more neutral soils. Many vegetables, for instance soybeans, corn, wheat, tomatoes, cucumbers, beans, strawberries, and squashes, do best at a pH of 6, which is the acidity of milk. Others prefer it closer to neutral. Carrots, peas, spinach, lettuce, onions, apples, cauliflower, beets, and asparagus are examples of those that do well in a pH range between 6 and 7, the latter being the equivalent of pure water. Sea water is slightly alkaline at pH 8 and soap solutions moderately so at pH 9. No common vegetables are comfortable at this end of the scale.

When the soil becomes alkaline, various minerals such as iron, manganese, and copper become tied up, or fixed in chemical compounds, and unavailable to plant roots. The plants may show symptoms of iron deficiency, or chlorosis (a yellowing). In such cases, the *new* leaves develop a light-yellow color which shows up first between the veins but gradually spreads to the veins as well. Similar is manganese deficiency where a chlorosis also appears between the veins on *new* leaves. With manganese deficiency, however, although this yellowing may spread to old leaves and while the chlorotic areas may turn brown or transparent, the veins usually remain green even in advanced stages.

We frequently see this chlorosis in our town on hydrangeas and rhododendrons, both of which, as we mentioned before, like slightly acid soils. These are often used as foundation plants close to stucco houses. Stucco has calcium in it, and this flakes off into the beds below and causes them to become alkaline. Under alkaline conditions the iron and manganese in the soil, plus any added by the gardener, without something like sulfur to increase acidity becomes fixed in compounds that cannot be absorbed by the plant roots. Thus the plants show iron or manganese deficiencies, even though a test of the soil might show plenty of those minerals. The soil scientist says in such cases that they are present but unavailable.

On the other hand, in acid soils iron, manganese, and aluminum all become easily available, sometimes in such quantities that they are actually toxic to the plants. Important macronutrients such as phosphorus may become fixed in compounds unavailable to plants in either acid or alkaline conditions, being most available to plants between pH 5.5 and pH 7.

This range, slightly more acid than neutral, also provides the best conditions for the growth of the bacteria that rot plant residues and those that take nitrogen out of the air and fix it in the soil. Both processes are essential in providing nutrients to plants.

What Have You Got?

How can you tell if your soil is acid or alkaline, or possesses the nutrients needed for plant growth?

Determining soil acidity is easy. Buy some PHydrion paper, make a solution of half water and half soil, dip the paper in the solution, and compare the color it turns with the chart that comes with the package. When we used such a field test in various different soils, we found it compared very favorably in accuracy with more sophisticated laboratory tests. (A good place to write for pH paper is Micro Essential Laboratory, Inc., Brooklyn, N.Y. 11210.) The cost for a roll of pH paper is between one and two dollars.

Be sure to buy a paper with a range from pH 3 or 4 to pH 9 or 10. If you keep the package in a moisture-proof container it will last many years. You may wish to test your soil at the end and beginning of each growing season, to learn how your rainfall or irrigation and fertilizing practices are affecting it. Organic matter has a buffering or stabilizing effect upon the soil solution. So if you are incorporating a great deal of compost into the soil, you may find the pH will change very little from time to time.

What if your soil turns out to be too acid for the plants

you want to grow? Add lime—dolomite limestone is the best as it breaks down slowly and contains both magnesium and calcium. Roughly 25 to 50 pounds for 1,000 square feet, or 1/2 to 5 pounds for 25 square feet. (See the chart on page 68, Using Lime to Correct Soil Acidity.)

The more clay and organic matter in your soil, the more lime it will take to change the pH. Remember, the pH scale is a logarithmic one, meaning that there are ten times more hydrogen ions at a pH of 4 than one of 5. Thus, to change the acidity from a pH of 5 to one of 6 will require less lime than moving it from pH 4 to pH 5.

Do not add lime to your compost pile. Although you will find books that recommend this, we have found that it will cause the pile to lose nitrogen in the form of ammonia, just what you *don't* want to happen.

To acidify an alkaline soil you can leach some of the salts away with water and add sulfur, which will be converted into acid by the sulfur-loving bacteria in the soil. Sulfur, by the way, is important for the development of plant and animal tissue. The addition of sulfur or lime to a soil may take several weeks to months to have full effect, so, if testing shows either necessary, you should make this one of the first steps in preparing your soil.

Once you are sure your soil is reasonably neutral, or in the favorable range, you can assume the nutrients already there are available to your plants. But how do you know what is there already and what is lacking? Two ways are often suggested in popular gardening books, but we have found neither one very useful for the urban gardener. Home test kits are frequently inaccurate, laboratory reports are very complex, and both may take sophisticated interpretation to be useful. What should you do? Here are three suggestions:

1. Learn to make a high-quality compost and use it plentifully and continually. If this compost contains a mixture

USING LIME TO CORRECT SOIL ACIDITY
Approximate amounts of finely ground limestone needed to raise the pH of a 7-inch layer of soil*

	Pounds of Limestone Added per 25 Square Feet		
Soil Regions and Textural Classes	From pH 3.5 to 4.5	From pH 4.5 to 5.5	From pH 5.5 to 6.5
Soils of Warm Temperate and Tropical Regions:			
Sand and loamy sand	.4	.4	.5
Sandy loam	—	.6	.8
Loam	—	1.0	1.3
Silt loam	—	1.5	1.8
Clay loam	—	1.9	2.5
Muck	3.0	4.0	4.8
Soils of Cool Temperate and Temperate Regions:			
Sand and loamy sand	.5	.6	.8
Sandy loam	—	1.0	1.7
Loam	—	1.5	2.1
Silt loam	—	1.9	2.5
Clay loam	—	2.4	2.9
Muck	3.6	4.8	5.4

*Calculated from U.S.D.A. Farmers' Bulletin No. 2124, *Liming Soils, An Aid to Better Farming*; 1.25 lbs. limestone/25 sq. ft. = 1 ton/acre.

NOTE: If you use quicklime instead of limestone, use 1/2 the amounts indicated, for hydrated lime about 3/4. These suggestions are based on soils of average organic matter content. For soils low in organic matter, reduce recommendations by 1/4; if high in organic matter, increase by 25%. Suggestions for muck soils are basically those free of sand and clay.

of kitchen garbage, grass, weeds, and leaves, you can assume it will provide a balance of nutrients for your plants through the decomposing action of soil macro- and micro-organisms.

2. Assume that nitrogen, because it is easily used by plants and easily leached away by water, will be in shortest supply. Add nitrogen to your compost and to your soil.

3. Learn to recognize symptoms of mineral deficiencies in your plants.

Nitrogen

Can you have too much nitrogen? Yes, you can. The plants will become large, weak, succulent-looking, and particularly attractive to aphids. There is more danger from too much nitrogen if you are adding it in inorganic, quickly-available compounds without adequate organic material in the soil, than if you are using organic sources as we are recommending in this book.

What is the cheapest and best source of nitrogen? Hold on to your hats, now . . . it's urine. That's right. That very stuff we and other animals produce every day in considerable quantities and flush away to cause waste management problems somewhere else—"Out of sight, out of mind."

Human urine is perfectly safe to use in the garden in the manner we are suggesting here. You need not fear that there is some pathogenic bacteria in the urine that could spread disease to another person, as can happen in the use of human feces for fertilizer. We checked this out very carefully before recommending our method to you. (Sterling Bunnell, M.D., personal communication; see also: Holprich, P.D., ed., *Infectious Diseases*, New York, Harper and Row, 1972, and Kaye, D., ed., *Urinary Tract Infection and its Management*, St. Louis, C.V. Mosby Co., 1972.)

The average daily output of urine is one to one and a half liters (1-3/4 to 2-7/8 pints) per day. In dry weight this is about forty to sixty grams (.09 to .13 pounds), and this contains 46.7 percent nitrogen. That means approximately fifteen grams of nitrogen in every liter of urine, or about twelve pounds of nitrogen per year per person. Enough to fertilize about 3,000 square feet at a rate of 200 pounds per acre.

The farmer commonly adds nitrogen in amounts of 100 to 300 pounds per acre. To add 200 pounds per acre by using your own urine, spread two quarts of urine for every twenty-seven square feet (three feet by nine feet) twice a month. If possible, dilute the urine five times with water in a sprinkling can. Urine is low in calcium but has a fair amount of salt which may be left in the soil. To help leach this away, once a year add approximately a quarter pound of lime or gypsum to every twenty-five square feet of soil. Dust it on the soil and water it in.

Now, we know perfectly well that confronting your own wastes is something our society finds very difficult. However, we are trying very faithfully to describe our own actual techniques and practices of growing food in the city. Hopefully we have not lost too many readers at this point by venturing into a taboo area.

Animal manures, as everyone knows, are a source of nitrogen. Poultry droppings are the highest in nitrogen, about 6 percent, since they contain urine and feces together. Fresh steer manure is good, usually about 2 percent. Horse manure may be very low because of the way it is obtained from many racing stables, mixed with so much bedding. It may use more nitrogen to decompose the mixture than the manure itself contributes. Rabbit manure may be sprinkled directly on the beds around the growing plants. We have seen a remarkably productive urban food garden that was fertilized this way almost exclusively. It could be called a "cold" manure because its nitrogen content is so low it will not burn plants as others can.

Two hundred pounds of nitrogen per acre is a little more than 1/10 of a pound per square foot. If a hundred-pound bag of steer manure is 2 percent nitrogen, that means, whether you haul or buy it, a hundred pounds of manure will contain only two pounds of nitrogen. That means you will need about five pounds for an area of twenty-five square feet (five feet by five feet). If you are buying nitrogen, be sure to take into account the percentage of each substance that you are actually paying for. A recent trip to the store showed nitrogen selling for anywhere from $.82 to $6.90 a pound. You will need to do some figuring to determine what is the best buy.

However, the best management system for all manures in the urban garden is to pass them through a fast compost pile. This will kill weed seeds as well as pathogenic or disease-causing organisms. This is a good way to handle dog manure and the contents of the kitty box.

For the rich and fastidious there are always blood meal and fish emulsions. Such substances are good sources of nitrogen and won't break the bank if you are using them in just a small area in the yard, or for a few houseplants. For the farmer, a good way to obtain nitrogen is to plant each field in clover, alfalfa, or other legumes every third or fourth year and turn it into the soil. This provides bacteria that are able to take nitrogen out of the air and fix it in the soil so that it is available to the plants that live in association with the roots of legume plants. But the average city gardener does not have the room to spare for this kind of crop rotation.

Recognizing Deficiencies

A book that may help you recognize symptoms of mineral deficiencies in your plants is *Hunger Signs in Crops* (a symposium, ed. Howard B. Sprague, New York: David McKay Co., 1964). This book has good pictures and a key for identifying symptoms. To understand the key they provide, it helps to realize that the minerals behave differently once they get inside the plants.

Potassium, for instance, is highly mobile. What little is available for the plant to use in building new tissues will be moved out of the old leaves and into the new. So potassium deficiencies show up first in the old leaves. To paraphrase the key in the book mentioned, these old leaves may turn an ashy gray, then develop a bronze or yellowish bronze color. The leaf margins may become brown and cup downward.

As mentioned earlier, iron and manganese deficiencies show up first in the new leaves. This is true of calcium also. This is because they are not very mobile nutrients when they are in the plant. Once fixed in the tissues they are not easily moved to new areas, even if the growing plant should later find itself in short supply. Calcium lack may show up as a yellowing or chlorosis of the new leaves, as do iron and manganese deficiencies. In addition, the tissues may break down at the blossom end of fruits. This can be seen on bell peppers rather easily. Vegetative growth may be retarded generally.

Lack of nitrogen and phosphorus may also retard the vegetative growth of the plant. But while nitrogen deficiency will cause a general paling and yellowing of the leaves (including veins), a lack of phosphorus may cause the leaves to be darker green than normal. In some vegetables the undersides of the leaves will develop a decided reddish-purplish hue. We realize all too well that these symptoms of plant deficiencies can easily be confused by the novice with equally colorful signs of plant disease and air pollution. When we first began studying the subject, we were able to muddle ourselves thoroughly in this respect!

Bill, with confidence, pointing to a plant actually suffering from a virus disease, "Ahh, this must be a sign of lack of nitrogen." Helga, uncertainly, "No, dear, don't you think it's an iron deficiency?" Bill, starting to feel a little shaky, "Let me see, that shows up in the old leaves first, doesn't it? Or . . . is it the new ones?"

We found that color pictures were a great help in learning to recognize what was what, as well as listening carefully to experts at the university and agricultural extension advisers, as they pointed out symptoms in actual plants that we brought in for them to diagnose. Another good way to learn symptoms of plant nutrient deficiencies is to purposely grow pots of plants where first one, and then another, of the major nutrients are deliberately eliminated from the soil mixture. The characteristic appearance of the various symptoms can then be memorized fairly easily.

The best information that we can give you about plant nutrients comes from discussions we've had with scientists in the soils and plant nutrition department of the University of California, Berkeley. Their advice: if you are using lots of well-made compost, plus some additional nitrogen, don't worry. On most soils, in most parts of the country, you should not need to add another single thing. Only a very small number of soils are so deficient in phosphorus that you need to worry about adding bone meal, or so short of potassium that kelp meal would be a good buy. Compost alone should provide enough of those minerals.

To sum it up then, compost, nitrogen—either from some animal manure or your own urine—and once a year the addition of a little lime should be all you ever need to grow good, healthy plants.

chapter 7

Carrots or Bok Choy?
Deciding What To Grow

"Let's start with staples," Bill said, surveying our first neatly cleared area—a generous expanse, six by six feet. "This is going to be a 'survival' food garden."

"You mean wheat?" was my astonished response.

For what should we use our precious little spot of ground? Poring over the seed catalogs left us more uncertain than before. The wealth of possibilities was greater than the ordinary supermarket shelves had led us to realize. Besides endless kinds of vegetables, there were varieties of each kind—dozens of squashes, loose-leaf and head lettuces, long and short carrots, etc. How were we to choose?

We needed to consider our purpose in growing some small part of our own diet.

Should we really grow staples? But potatoes, dry beans, and such were relatively cheap and available, even in organic food stores. Should we grow delicacies that are expensive to buy? Leeks, which sit in the ground a long time, forcing chicory, which takes a lot of handling, sugar peas, which must be picked as they mature to keep the plant producing, are some examples. Should we grow exotic vegetables because they're difficult or impossible to buy in the store? There are catalogs that offer Chinese, Japanese, and European vegetables and spices. Maybe freshness should be a consideration. The flavor of sweet corn, uncooked, eaten right off the stalk, beets pulled then cooked a few seconds later, and tomatoes ripened on the vine are infinitely more delicious than the same vegetables after they've traveled the long road from the farm to you, and their sugars have begun to change to starches.

One of our own reasons for raising food was to avoid consuming so much pesticide. Thus, heavily sprayed vegetables such as strawberries and lettuce, and those that absorb pesticides from the ground, such as carrots, were among our first choices. How about nutrition? The dark green leaf lettuces have more vitamins and minerals, but my son likes only crispy head lettuce. What about growing something during the warm part of the year that you can eat in the winter? Winter squash, Jerusalem artichokes, string beans for freezing, and tomatoes for canning all sounded great.

The truth is, over the years, whether on the rooftop or in miscellaneous spaces around the house, we've tried raising nearly everything at least once. This way we learned firsthand what suited our taste, our miniclimate, soil, space, methods of gardening, and the amount of time we were willing to spare.

Taste is a personal matter and one not easily influenced. People tend to accept foods they grew up with, but may be very conservative about trying or liking something new. Eating too much of a thing for a while, no matter how much you liked it originally, may influence your feelings about it for a long time. During the first years of our urban farm we ate so much chard, because it grew so lustily in our unimproved clay soil, that we don't feel much enthusiasm for it any more. Yet it takes up a disproportionate amount of the yard just because it seeds itself so readily. If you hope to enlist the hearty participation of other members of your household in your urban gardening venture, it would be best if you start out growing things they actually like to eat!

We have already discussed how miniclimate and soils will affect your plantings. Now let's take a closer look at those other constraints of the urban gardener—space and time.

Not Much Space?

Here are some approaches to making the best use of whatever small amount of space you may have.

1. Start your seedlings indoors, if possible. Chapter 8 tells you how. That way, space will not be taken up in the garden by plants during their first weeks of life when they can do just fine on the window sill. This is particularly important in those parts of the country where a long growing season means that several crops can be harvested in a single season.

2. Plant "cut and come again" vegetables. Once the plant has become established, loose-leaf lettuce and sprouting broccoli will continue to furnish small amounts of harvest every few days over a long period of time. In the same amount of ground space pole beans or peas will many times out-produce their bush-type relatives. Jerusalem artichokes, besides being generally more indestructible than potatoes as plants, will yield many times the amount of tubers in the same depth of soil. They can be prepared in all the ways that potatoes can, besides being edible raw in salads and a nice substitute for crisp water chestnuts in Chinese dishes. They are also good for the dieter who is avoiding extra calorie intake. Compact varieties of winter squash (grown in the summer and, because of their thick water-repelling skins, stored for winter eating) form a bush that will give you the same amount of food close to the main stem that older varieties will produce while sprawling over many square feet of precious ground. Golden Nugget is one such variety. A careful reading of the seed catalogs will alert you to the most compact varieties of the vegetables you have chosen to grow.

3. Make use of or build structures that take advantage of vertical space. Cucumbers, squashes, tomatoes, peas, and beans can all be made to grow up if they are adequately

supported. As large, heavy winter squashes form, they may need additional support.

Strawberries can be grown in "step" containers. This makes it possible to set many plants in the same ground area while still providing adequate root space. The berries are kept drier and are less subject to rot and attack by pests. Harvest is easy and the runners can be managed very well in this arrangement.

4. Where you have no open ground, use containers on

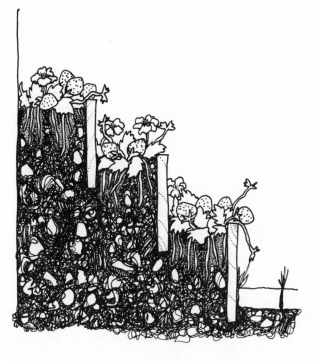

"Step" containers allow
for more plants in an area
or volume of soil. (cut-away view)

patios or the roof, on unused walks or driveways, in window boxes, on shelves or tables inside the house in a sunny window. Some plants will do particularly well this way. Summer squashes, for instance, seem to thrive under conditions that simulate the arid Southwest where bitter wild squashes still live. Give them a roomy container so that their roots can enjoy moisture at the same time the vines trail over a hot, dry surface. A friend's bumper crop of zucchini was grown in an old double washtub set in one corner of a cement parking area.

5. Interplant slow-growing vegetables with those that will be harvested in a short time. Radishes, turnips, and lettuce will be gone before corn or cabbage becomes large enough to use all the ground space it ultimately needs. The seed catalogs usually tell you the approximate time to ma-

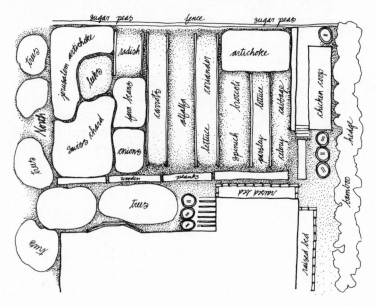

backyard winter garden

turity of each variety. Although the actual number of days to harvest will depend largely on the weather, the relative times between varieties will be a good guide to learning which vegetables to interplant with which.

6. Plant tall things at the north side of your spot so that you do not lose growing space to unnecessary shading.

7. Make large beds with few walkways. Remember, you're not setting up an area to be cultivated with a tractor! This is the main reason that a small urban garden can be so productive if calculated in terms of yield per acre. No space needs to be wasted for, or destroyed by, vehicle traffic. The beds should be just the width that makes it possible to reach comfortably to the center from each side; the walkways or stepping areas just frequent enough and wide enough to make everything convenient and accessible.

In our garden, we follow the "jungle" style of garden layout. Since more than half of our vegetables are left to seed themselves in, they naturally tend to ignore human conveniences such as paths. So, to maneuver about, you must clamp your sun hat firmly to your head, clasp your picking basket tightly, and take flying leaps, or, often, circle half-way round the yard to reach a succulent something. Horribly disorderly, but heavenly productive!

Time: A Big Villain

The other major constraint of the urban gardener is time. This has several dimensions. It's very unlikely that, if you live in the city, you can devote most of your time to agriculture. How much time you want to give to raising some of your own food is one aspect of the time question. The others are: how much of the year can you grow food *in*, which, as we saw in Chapter 3, is only partly a function of climate, and how much of the year can you grow food *for*, which is a matter of food preservation.

Certain gardening techniques we use are great time savers. Some have already been mentioned.

1. Use compost mulches to keep down weeds, decrease frequency of watering, and keep soil soft.

2. Start seedlings indoors on the window sill or a sunny table. This way, when you come home from work and you are tired and it's getting dark, you will not have to drag yourself outside to water your seedlings. Also, you get a head start on wildlife that might wipe them out in a single gulp. (More about this later.)

However, perhaps it's best to interject one comment about bug problems here, since it deals with time. If you

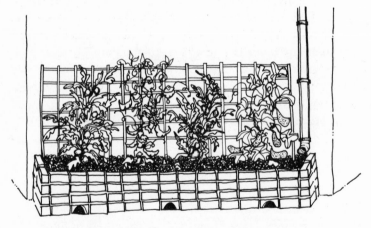

front view - long narrow raised bed
drain pipe from roof top.
holes at bottom for drainage

don't want to use pesticides you will have to spend time on alternate methods of pest management. They may be just as successful as pesticides or more so, but they will take more time, attention, and information. Remember, the appeal of the push-button poisons was that they seemed to promise a *quick* and *easy* method of controlling bugs!

3. Use overhead water methods. Get a large rectangular sprinkler that can cover the whole area you are planting all at once. When you have determined its pattern, amount of coverage, and allowed for prevailing winds, leave it in one place with the hose connected. As your plants grow taller, you may wish to elevate it on a box.

The weekly watering, when necessary, is then a simple chore. Go out, turn on the hose, set your timer, and when it rings, turn the water off. If each planting area is arranged with its own watering system, you can save a great deal of time. The water draining from our rooftop containers flows down a drainpipe to soak a raised bed below. Extra moisture lovers, such as chives, mint, or celery, can be planted beneath faucets and by hose connections, so as to take advantage of the extra drips that are bound to be available.

We talked about extending the growing season with mini-greenhouses and other devices in Chapter 3. Let's consider here how to extend the use of the food you grow by preserving it.

Preserving Food While Preserving the Planet

The question is, how can you preserve food while preserving the planet too?

Let's consider first those methods that don't depend heavily on artificial sources of energy.

Drying is one of the old successful ways of keeping food. Without the moisture necessary to all life, even the bacteria that cause spoilage cannot grow. Herbs should be cut before they go to flower and stored in a cool shady place inside paper bags to dry. When they are dry and crumbly, brush off the leaves and keep in tightly covered jars away from light.

Fruit—apricots, apples, pears, plums, grapes, figs, domestic and wild berries—can all be dried in the sun if your days are dry and hot enough. Spread the fruit out in one layer on a tray; window screens are perfect for this. When possible we elevate the screens so that air can flow under as well as over the drying food. You may want to cover the fruit with cheesecloth if you seem to be attracting flies or birds. See Chapter 10 for ideas about excluding ants. To obtain plans for building a home solar dryer, write the Natural Energy Design Center, Sim van der Ryn, Department of Agriculture, University of California, Berkeley.

Once you have stored dried fruits, grains, and nuts, protecting them from insects is another problem. From the booklet *Common Pantry Pests and their Control*, published by the University of California Agricultural Extension Service, comes the following advice:

> Both low and high temperatures can control food pests. Insect activity ceases at temperatures of 40° to 50° F. Prolonged exposure to a temperature of 40° F will kill most food insects, and even the most resistant are killed within three weeks, if placed in a deep freeze. An exposure of two to three days will kill the more susceptible species which make up the greatest number that attack stored products. Food materials stored at this temperature will remain free of infestation.
>
> To kill all stages of insect life in stored products, expose to temperatures of 120° to 130° F for two hours. However, the insect itself must be subjected to the heat for the required time. Be sure to reach

and maintain the proper temperature at the center of the material being treated. To insure rapid heat penetration, spread the material in as thin a layer as possible and stir it from time to time. (Heat may be injurious to protein quality, so this method should be reserved for luxury items that are used for reasons other than the nutrition they offer—pine nuts would be an example.)

You can sterilize (disinfect) small quantities in an oven, but be careful not to scorch the product. In many cases you can obtain the desired temperature by merely turning up the pilot light in a gas oven. A longer exposure may be necessary for sufficient heat penetration.

If you use the oven, keep the temperature as low as possible; the usual resulting temperature of 180° F will cause a rapid kill. You may open the oven door slightly to keep the temperature from rising too high. Use a thermometer to check the temperature increase.

To kill insects infesting dried fruits, drop the fruit in boiling water for about one minute. Spread the fruit to dry before storing.

Carbon dioxide can be used to treat and preserve walnut and other nut meats. You can obtain it as dry ice (solid carbon dioxide). See classified section in telephone book.

Crack out the nut kernels. If they are not fully dried, spread them out in a thin layer (not in the sun) until dry and brittle. The drier they are the better their quality after storage.

Put a single layer of kernels in the bottom of the jars.

Cut one-inch cubes of dry ice. A common wood saw is satisfactory for this purpose. A five-pound dry ice slab, ten inches by ten inches by one inch will make 100 pieces.

Put a dry ice cube on the layer of kernels a short distance from the side of the jar where it can be

seen after the jar is full. (Jars may crack if the dry
ice is against the glass.) Use about one-half cubic
inch of dry ice for pint jars, one cubic inch for
one-quart jars, and two cubic inches for two-quart
jars.

Fill with kernels, shake down—fill as full as possible. A quart jar will hold twelve to fourteen
ounces.

Put on the lids and screw them down until they
begin to tighten. Then turn them back until slightly loose. Lids must be loose to allow the air and
excess gas to escape and to prevent explosion of
the jars.

Allow jars to stand undisturbed until all dry ice is
gone.

Screw lids down tightly.

Store in as cool a place as possible.

Caution: Do not handle dry ice with bare
hands—it will freeze the skin quickly. Wear gloves.

Do not seal the jars until all dry ice has disappeared.

Waxing the stem ends of squashes may help them store
for a longer period without drying or rotting. In frontier
northern California, vegetables such as cabbages, carrots,
and beets were stored in sawdust—sometimes in sheds especially constructed for the purpose. Eggs were stored in
"waterglass" or concentrated sodium silicate. A close
friend, describing her childhood experiences with this technique on her parent's ranch, told how in summer, freshly
laid eggs would be stored away in large covered crocks in a
cool room to be used for baking in the winter. She empha-
sized, though, that waterglassed eggs were not flavorful
enough to use scrambled or in similar dishes where a fresh
egg taste was desirable.

The important thing in storing food is to keep it at the
correct temperature, humidity, and ventilation. Two excellent booklets which give you detailed information on this

zyme action before freezing. Others can be frozen directly; particularly good results can be obtained with tomatoes, green peppers, and blueberries.

Even frozen foods cannot be kept in good condition forever. You need to keep track of what you've got and eat the oldest foods first. Most freezers come with directions on freezing foods. The USDA puts out some good booklets on this also. Maybe right here we should suggest you write for the *List of Available Publications* from the USDA. You will find plenty of information as useful for the urban gardener as for the rural homesteader.

Some last words about freezing. The bin-type freezer uses a lot less energy than the upright cabinet. That's because every time you open the door of the upright, the cold air, which is heavy, flows out and sinks to the floor, while it pretty much stays put in a bin. Keeping the freezer in a cool place is a good idea also. Then it won't have to work so hard keeping the contents cold. If you want an upright refrigerator-freezer combination, choose one without automatic defrosting equipment—this latter uses a lot more energy than the other kinds.

Eventually we had to ask ourselves some hard questions about our urban farm. We didn't have much space, much of the space we did have didn't have much light with only half-day sun, and we had very little time to give to our food raising. What part of our diet could we realistically hope to supply through growing our own food?

This question really breaks down into two parts—quantity and quality.

Quantity, or Counting Calories

Quantity in our diet is best looked at in terms of calories. Again, we depend heavily on government booklets for our information. The National Research Council of the National Academy of Sciences has published tables that show the daily calorie input they recommend for children, men, and women of different ages. These cannot be taken as absolutes, for they do not include individual variations in metabolism, physical labor, physique, etc. But they are very valuable as a general framework for putting your garden produce in perspective. For women the recommendations range from a peak consumption of 2,400 calories per day for 14 to 16 year olds, to 1,700 per day for those over 55 years. For men, from 3,000 calories per day to 2,400 are suggested for roughly the same age spans.

Armed with this perspective, we turned to a very informative book, *Composition of Foods*, Agricultural Handbook #4, published by the USDA. We learned some interesting things. For instance, a hundred grams (or 3½ ounces) of the following foods yielded very different amounts of calories. (All but the first two were among the foods we raised around our house.)

Hard red spring wheat, cooked	168 cal./100 gms.
Brown rice, cooked	119 cal./ "
Lima beans, cooked	111 cal./ "
Fava or broad beans, immature, raw	105 cal./ "
Potatoes, baked	93 cal./ "
boiled	73 cal./ "
Sweet corn, boiled on the cob	91 cal./ "
Green peas, raw	84 cal./ "
cooked, boiled, drained	71 cal./ "
Jerusalem artichokes, just harvested	7 cal./ "
stored for a week	75 cal./ "
Squash, (all varieties, acorn highest) baked	63 cal./ "
boiled	38 cal./ "
Beets, boiled	32 cal./ "

| Broccoli, boiled | 26 cal./ " |
| Green beans, boiled | 25 cal./ " |

We could go on with a complete list, but since it is already available in the book just mentioned, we suggest you get a copy for yourself and look up the foods you are, or intend to be, growing.

The missing information, and this we cannot supply you with at this time, is how many grams or ounces of each food can be grown in a given amount of space in a backyard garden. While yield figures are available for agricultural crops, they have not been computed for backyard gardeners. We suspect that on a per-acre basis they could very well be higher than that achieved in commercial agriculture. This seems likely because of the intensive care and more complete utilization of the harvest in a small garden than can be economically accomplished on a large scale. We don't need to leave space for tractor wheels and we harvest every tomato, for instance. On the other hand, backyard gardens may have less than perfect light conditions and city gardeners may be ignorant of plant nutritional needs, both of which may severely limit production.

It is plain from the above table, however, that next to grains, it is the beans, potatoes, peas, and corn that are real winners, with winter squashes not too far behind. In fact, beans, corn, and squash formed the basis of many American Indian diets on this continent long before western Europeans arrived.

Quality

But quantity is only part of the nutrition story. It is also necessary to consider quality. You may think first of protein, but quality can also be applied to vitamins and minerals.

All of us have been impressed with the importance of

protein by teachers and breakfast cereal manufacturers alike. But knowing how much protein a given food contains tells you little about how much of the protein is usable by your body. There are eight amino acids (building blocks of protein) we must consume because the human body cannot synthesize them, and they must be present in specific proportions in relation to each other to be totally usable. Thus, though a given amount of milk may have much less protein in it than the same amount of soybeans, more of the milk protein is usable because the pattern of those eight necessary amino acids more nearly approximates the ideal for human consumption. A chicken egg is considered to have the ideal proportion of amino acids most useful to humans, but dairy products are not far behind, and after that comes meat. (We will discuss the raising of chickens and rabbits in a later chapter.)

At this point in our own inquiry into garden sources of protein, we encountered Frances Moore Lappé's excellent book, *Diet for a Small Planet* (New York: Friends of the Earth/Ballantine Books, 1971). We recommend that you read this book if you wish to make the best use of your garden-produced plant protein. The story is a complicated one, and we will not take the space to repeat it here. In sum, we eventually realized that the way to make the best use of the fairly large quantity of low-quality protein available to us in the beans and peas we could produce would be to combine them with the dairy products that we buy. While grains and nuts also contain some protein, these might be difficult for urban gardeners to produce.

Our conclusion: unless you are raising your own rabbits or chickens (both entirely possible for many urban gardeners, but themselves partially dependent on outside sources of feed), or producing a lot of soybeans and lima beans, the protein contribution to your diet by your urban garden will have to be heavily supplemented with dairy products and grains to provide the necessary nutritional balance.

Vitamins and minerals are another matter, however. Vegetables are major contributors in this area. Since vitamins can be lost through careless storage, handling, or cooking, observe these rules:

1. Eat your vegetables as soon as possible after cooking.

2. Eat as many vegetables raw, or barely cooked, as you can learn to enjoy in that form.

3. Do not soak or excessively rinse vegetables ahead of cooking.

4. Cook in as little water as possible.

5. Expose to the air as little as possible during cooking. (Don't keep lifting the pot lid to peek in.)

6. Use the liquid in which you cooked the vegetables.

We found Chinese-style stir-fried foods have much to recommend them besides a low consumption of fuel energy for cooking. The vegetables are pre-cut, then heated quickly in a small amount of oil and eaten while still crisp. A variety of vegetables can go in the pot at once, enabling the home gardener to make use of whatever is ready for harvest at the moment. Few vitamins are lost from overcooking or wasted juices, and, if you are using meat, a small amount goes a very long way.

Even shady gardens or shallow containers can produce excellent greens for stir-frying (and the weeds can feed meat rabbits). We have used many varieties of Chinese cabbage (Chinese celery cabbage or Petsai, Wong-bok, Chinese cabbage Hirasuka, Pac-choy—all available from Nichols Garden Nursery, 1190 N. Pacific Hwy., Albany, Oregon 97321). Spinach, lettuce, regular green and rhubarb chard, mustard greens, kale and collards, upland cress, New Zealand spinach, parsley, coriander, and green onions have all gone into lovely stir-fried dishes. We have grown them all successfully in less than perfect light conditions and in containers from eight inches to one foot deep. Of course, this style of cooking also lends itself well to incorporating the many vegetables that require sun and deeper soils to produce.

Thus, by buying only brown rice and a few additions like sesame seeds, soy sauce, peanut oil, and ginger (and a little alfalfa supplement for the rabbits), we found that within three months of starting our urban farm we could proudly and truthfully say that a goodly portion of the food on the table we had produced ourselves.

chapter 8

Starting with Seeds

You've planned your urban garden to make best use of your miniclimate, decided what you want to grow, learned about your soil and how to improve it, and, hopefully, started your first batch of compost with which to prepare the beds. Now you are ready to order seeds and plant.

When we started our urban garden we went to a local supermarket and picked up a handful of seed packages—carrots, beets, lettuce, broccoli. If we thought about varieties we assumed that the store would naturally be carrying the kinds most suitable for our climate, and this is generally true. Then we discovered seed catalogs (they are usually free), and our real education began.

There are seed companies in Wisconsin and some in Georgia, as well as what seems like every other state in the union. Some specialize in trees, some in herbs, some in Japanese vegetables, some in honey plants to feed bees. There are English catalogs which carry many varieties particularly suited to our West Coast climate and American catalogs with vegetables from Europe and the Orient. Because peas, beans, and some other seeds are very susceptible to fungus attacks, some companies treat their seeds with fungicide. If you follow our method of starting plants, you will not need this precaution. If you do not wish to use treated seed, you must specify that with your order. There are catalogs with color photos or etchings which are so beautiful you could hang them on the wall, and there are others with no pictures at all where the same seeds are half the price or less, but you need to have a picture in your mind of what you want.

Perhaps the biggest surprise for us was the discovery that

there are so many varieties of most common types of vegetables. Many of these we had never seen in the stores because they just don't pack and ship well, or for some other reason they have not become popular with growers or distributors. For instance, we learned there were not only head lettuces and loose-leaf lettuces, but types in between, with many more leaf shapes and colors than we had ever imagined.

How To Study Seed Catalogs

There are several things to keep in mind when reading a seed catalog. First, notice how many days are listed as "days to maturity." This figure refers to approximately the number of days from planting to harvest (unless the catalog specifies otherwise). Of course this number is not absolute, because weather will vary from year to year as well as in different parts of the country, but by comparing one variety with another, you will get a good impression of the relative speed with which the different ones mature. Beans, for instance, may vary in time from planting to harvest from fifty-five days for some bush beans, seventy days for some varieties of pole beans, to ninety days for some limas. Radishes, from twenty-two days for the early round red ones to sixty days for the Chinese long white ones, and so on.

Knowing this is valuable. If you live in areas with a short season, it is obviously essential to plant varieties that will mature before your first fall frosts. Secondly, in areas with longer seasons, by planting both early and late varieties you are able to stretch out your harvest period for that particular vegetable.

This is also the reason for making careful choices between those seeds described as "market" varieties, meaning they will mature their fruits all at the same time (so that you can take a load to sell in the market), and "home garden" or "old fashioned" varieties which ripen fruits every few days over a long period. You probably don't want to eat salad cucumbers morning, night, and noon. On the other hand, it might be desirable to have a lot of pickling cucumbers ready all at once so that when you get out the canning equipment, you can put up a big batch of pickles at one time.

Check the description to find out if the vegetable is a bush variety, climber, or—this is particularly important with squashes in a small garden—whether it is a compact type. Also consider disease resistance. If this is the first time you are planting any vegetables in a particular soil, you may escape some of the fungus and virus diseases which tend to build up slowly over the years in each locality before problems become noticeable. But sometimes it's good to check with vegetable-growing neighbors regarding disease problems they might have observed in your area.

Another factor to consider is storing qualities. Onions and winter squashes are two vegetables you may wish to grow and keep for months during the winter without re-frigeration, and the varieties differ in their ability to keep well. Potatoes are another vegetable you may wish to store if you have the space in which to produce them. Before modern refrigeration was available, root crops such as carrots, beets, and parsnips, as well as cabbages, were all stored for the winter in root cellars, tucked away in leaves or sawdust. It would be a very unusual inner-city gardener who could produce enough extra to take advantage of this possibility. However, for suburban gardeners whose lots and energies are great enough, it would be worthwhile to check the seed catalogs for the keeping qualities of these vegetables.

Notice also whether the vegetable is a hybrid. These specially fertilized seeds will combine the best qualities of both parent plants, but usually cannot be relied upon to pass on all their good traits in the same proportions to their offspring. So, plant hybrids where you want the special characteristics of vigor, color, taste, yields, disease resistance, etc., and plan to give them the careful fertilization and care that they will demand to produce the results for which they are noted.

Members of the brassica or cabbage family (cabbage, broccoli, cauliflower, kohlrabi, Brussels sprouts, collards, mustard greens, radishes, turnips, rutabagas, Chinese or Napa cabbage, etc.) and the cucurbits (cucumbers, squashes, and melons) are difficult to raise from home-produced seed in any case, since they tend to interbreed within their own family. So they would be good choices for hybrid varieties. But for those vegetables you will not have much time to fuss over, or from which you plan to save the seed (and this can be done profitably with nearly all seeds, except for cucurbits and brassicas), it is best to choose nonhybrid or old fashioned varieties. So many of these will even seed themselves in, if you keep a mulched garden as we do.

Saving Your Own Seeds

We have had particular luck with saving our own seeds from peas, beans, carrots, onions (they will flower the second season), lettuce, coriander, New Zealand spinach, chard, cooking celery, parsley, upland cress, and tomato. With most of the above you can either collect the seed from the dried flower head, or, as in the case of chard, keep the entire branchlet of seed pods stored for the winter. With tomatoes you'll need to mash away the pulp from the seeds. Then dry them thoroughly, spread out on a paper towel or screen, before you store them away.

All seeds, whether bought or saved from your own garden, should be kept in a cool, dry place. This is essential as you want seeds that will germinate with vigor the following season.

If you plan to save some of your own seeds, be attentive to which plants you are choosing for this purpose. Always select the best individual plant with the specific characteristics you desire, as the one from which to save the seeds. Mark it with a stake or red ribbon or something, early in the season, so that it will get good care and not be harvested by mistake.

There is great genetic variation among the seeds of each variety of plant. By selecting year after year the individuals that most satisfy your particular desires, you will gradually develop a type that is particularly well suited to your climate, soil, care, and palate.

Planting Indoors

When we began our urban garden we started all our seeds directly in the ground. It was very exciting to rush home after work to give the seedbeds a watering and go out again in the morning to make sure they stayed moist enough for the day. However, we began to suffer some losses almost at once. During the day, birds flocked to our lettuce, carrot, and corn seedlings. At night cutworms cut the slender stalks at ground level and left the entire seedling lying there to betray their presence. Slugs and snails are tremendous pests in our area and they would mow down several feet of row in a single evening.

We were putting so much attention on our new venture that every bite by a wild animal seemed like a large-scale tragedy. We took to building screens to keep out birds, using collars against cutworms, putting down sawdust, and night handpicking with a flashlight to foil our wildlife visitors.

After a while, the novelty wore off. Hovering over the seedlings became another chore to attend to in the midst of an already too demanding schedule of jobs and volunteer activities. There had to be an easier way!

We started raising our seedlings indoors and putting them outside when they were large enough to go without attention for a couple of days at a stretch. We used commercially sold peat pots, but they were expensive. We tried egg shells—too small. That is, they were all right if you planted the seedling as soon as it was ready to go into the ground, but for busy persons like us, it was not uncommon for several weeks to go by, and by that time the seedling was either dead or permanently stunted by being in such cramped quarters. Then we tried miscellaneous cartons, such as those that cottage cheese comes in, but it was too hard to get the seedlings out without damaging the root hairs.

Finally, after considerable experimentation, we developed the method we shall describe here step by step. We've taught this technique to hundreds of people. It's just about fool-proof, even for children.

We have started every type of vegetable this way, even those that supposedly don't like transplanting, and we've had good luck moving them to the garden later. This method has many advantages. It uses seed economically, the little trays fit neatly on the window sill, the young seedlings are not exposed to drying by winds or attack by wild animals (though we have had a few catastrophes with a kitten learning to climb), they are easy to check on morning and night, and you will have a jump on the season as you would with a greenhouse or a cold frame.

Materials

1. A sunny window.
2. Quart-sized milk cartons—one carton will make

three cube-shaped containers which can hold a total of four seedlings each. Thus, a total of twelve plants can be raised in a one-quart milk carton.

3. Half-gallon-sized milk cartons—one carton will make two trays. Each tray will hold two cube-shaped containers.

4. Soil—if your soil is very loose and sandy, mix it with a little peat moss or compost. If your soil is a heavy clay, you'll need to add sand and peat moss or compost. A good mixture is: 1/3 sand, 1/3 soil, and 1/3 peat moss or compost. You can use peat moss, but sifted compost is best. Peat moss and sand can be bought in a plant nursery. (Beach sand is too salty.) Compost can be made out of your kitchen wastes, grass clippings, leaves, sawdust, etc.

5. Seeds—if the vegetables you are growing now are not hybrids, you can save and use the seeds of lettuce, onions, carrots, swiss chard, New Zealand spinach, leeks, parsley, coriander, upland cress, tomatoes, celery, asparagus, peas, and beans. Do not attempt to save the seeds from members of the cabbage family (broccoli, cauliflower, cabbage, kohlrabi, radish, turnips, rutabaga, Brussels sprouts, collards, kale, mustard greens, etc.) or the cucurbits (melons, squash, cucumbers). Store all seeds in a cool, dry place. Don't try to save them more than one season.

6. Scissors and a sharp knife for cutting cartons; toothpicks and scraps of paper for labels; a stapler (optional); and a container for mixing soil. A flexible plastic bowl is good.

Procedure

1. Cut each quart-sized milk carton into three open-ended cubes. Cut off the top and bottom of carton. Cut twice through the carton to get thirds.

2. Cut each half-gallon milk carton in half the long

way, to make two trays. On the half where the end has been opened to make a pouring spout, staple it closed. Or, if you have plenty of cartons, just discard the opened side (it will leak).

3. Mix sand, soil, and peat moss or compost together thoroughly.

4. Set two open-ended cube-shaped containers into each tray. Fill almost up to the top with the dry soil mixture. (By squeezing the plastic bowl you can form a pouring spout for the soil.)

5. Pack down the soil firmly, using the back of fingers and knuckles—there should be a half-inch of space between soil surface and top of carton.

6. Soak soil by pouring water into center of soil surface. This should create a little depression in center. Add enough water so that cartons are standing in about 1/4 inch of water.

7. Let soil stand and soak up the water.

8. Make a depression with your finger in each corner of the wet soil surface.

9. Drop two or three seeds into each corner depression.

10. Cover with clean sand, just enough to exclude light *but no deeper*. (Disregard what the seed package says. Seeds started indoors are in an environment that is darker and warmer than outdoors, and thus more subject to fungus disease.) Lettuce seeds may be left uncovered.

11. Write out a label on a scrap of paper and mount it on a toothpick.

12. Check the containers every morning and night. If the surface dries out, add a *little* water by pouring it into center depression—just enough to wet the surface. Seeds must be kept damp while germinating, but too much moisture will encourage disease.

13. When seedlings appear, move the carton to a sunny window.

14. If more than one seedling appears in a corner, wait until the first leaves appear. Then choose the best looking seedling (biggest leaves, toughest stem, best color green) and cut off (don't pull out) other seedlings competing with it.

15. Keep seedlings damp as they grow.

16. They are ready to transplant outdoors or to a larger container when they get their second or "true" leaves. However, if compost has been used in the soil mixture, there should be enough nutrients present to continue letting the seedlings grow in the same container another week or two before moving them.

Note—How often you need to water will depend on the kind of organic material you use and on how warm and dry your house is. If the soil mixture contains a good sifted compost, the house is kept fairly cool (68°F), and the planting mix was thoroughly soaked to begin with, watering once a week may be all that is necessary.

These are the advantages to the urban gardener of starting seedlings indoors: It is easy to protect seedlings from bugs, birds, and other wildlife, while they are young and tender. It is easy to keep them damp enough. The plants won't take up space in the garden during the three to six weeks or so that they are very tiny. You can start the plants earlier in the year, if the weather outdoors is still pretty cold at night. You can transplant the seedlings to the exact distance apart desired and they won't need to go through a thinning process. It is fun to watch closely as the seedlings grow—if you come home late and tired from work and it may be dark and cold outside, your seedlings are still easily accessible to you on your window sill. And finally, it uses seeds economically.

Outdoors

Eventually, after a couple of years of starting everything indoors, we began to modify our routine somewhat. We found that starting seeds outdoors and then thinning out what we didn't want was in some cases easier than starting them inside. We learned to let some vegetables just seed themselves in by themselves.

We now plant our carrots outdoors right away. First we prepared, with wooden boards for sides, a raised bed of 1/3 sifted dirt (ours is a heavy clay), 1/3 sand we bought at a sand and gravel company (specify fresh water sand), and 1/3 sifted compost. (We also originally added bone meal as a number of books pointed out how important phosphorus was for carrots. Then we learned that our soil was not deficient in that mineral and the compost was providing plenty anyway.) Then we scattered the seeds as evenly as possible all over the bed.

Since we save our old carrot flower heads when they are full of mature (dry) seeds, this means crushing these in our hands and letting the pieces of stalks fall with the seeds themselves. Next we cover everything with a thin layer of sifted compost and water it down thoroughly. Finally, we stretch strips of burlap tightly over the beds, securing them with tacks into the board sides. The burlap does not touch the surface of the beds, leaving a space of at least two

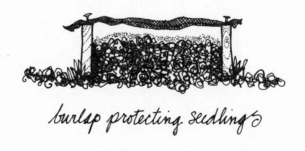

burlap protecting seedlings

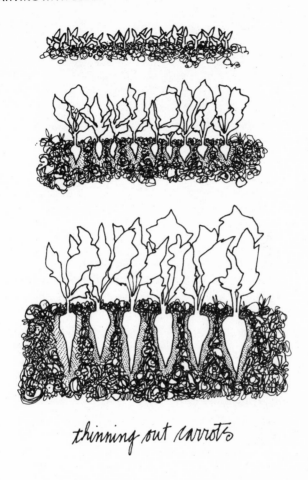

thinning out carrots

inches for the growth of the little seedlings. This way we shade the beds and prevent them from drying out, so that watering is only necessary every other day or less. The thin compost mulch on top of the seeds helps to keep them moist also.

When the seedlings appear, we start periodic thinning. The baby carrots are good to eat if you have the patience to wash off the soil. In any case, the rabbits love them. Eventually, we give each carrot at least an inch and a half

chicken wire protection from birds

all around, by thinning out the largest ones as the carrots grow. We protect the beds from birds by chicken-wire tunnels that we have made until the seedlings are large enough not to be so attractive. Our cats help us in this respect also.

We also start peas and beans outside, first soaking them overnight to get them started. (The quicker you can get them above the ground and growing, the less likely you are to lose them to the fungus disease to which they are very susceptible.) Each time we plant these legumes where to our knowledge there have been no members of that family growing before, we inoculate them with a mix of bacteria, commonly sold by nurseries and seed catalogs as "legume aid."

There is a group of bacteria, each particular to different members of the legume family, that live in close association with the roots of the plants and are able to take nitrogen out of the air and change it to make it available to plants as a fertilizer. This is the reason that clover, vetches, and other legumes are planted by farmers as a green "manure." For the soil to receive the full benefit of this nitrogen production, it is necessary to turn the entire plant into the soil at the end of the season. When the plant and bacteria associated with it die and decompose, their bodies release the nitrogen for other plants to use. However, while it is alive, the plant receives benefits from these bacteria, and the results are visible in the greater yields produced by those plants that were inoculated compared to those that were not treated.

The spores, or resting stages, of these bacteria tend to remain for years in the soil where they were introduced, so it is not necessary to inoculate legumes going into soil where they were grown once before. In fact, it is possible to build up a soil bank of these bacteria and simply mix each batch of legume seeds that will go into a new area with soil from where inoculated beans or peas were grown the year before. You can tell if your soil has the bacteria present in any quantity already by pulling up a legume plant and inspecting it for the conspicuous nodules, or lumps, that the plant creates to house these "nitrogen-fixers."

Loose-leaf lettuce seeds are another group we grow directly in the ground outdoors. Some seeds itself in each year. New varieties we sow by scattering the seeds thinly over the mulch in one or another of our big planter boxes and watering them in. Since lettuce will germinate in the light, there is no need to cover them over.

Corn we also seed directly in the ground and protect with chicken wire when it is small. This is one plant that demands a great deal of nitrogen. Regular monthly urine waterings, high-quality steer manure or blood meal, plus a well-made compost, are absolute musts for getting a good crop.

If your preference is for starting other seeds outdoors, you can find ample directions for doing so on seed packages and in government pamphlets and garden books; therefore we will not take the space here for a description of the planting requirements of each vegetable. All the other vegetables we start inside and transplant outdoors when they are large enough.

When and How to
Transplant

If you are following our methods of starting seedlings indoors in milk cartons, you will usually have a space of several weeks' leeway in getting seedlings into the ground. They must not be disturbed until they have gotten their second pair of leaves, or first pair of "true" leaves. These usually look different from the leaves that emerge from the seed. The trick is to transplant the seedling sometime between that point and the time they get too large for the container, thus running out of root space and nutrients.

A few days to a week before you plan to set them in the ground outside, the seedlings need to be "hardened off." This means getting them used to the different outdoor temperatures, wind, and moisture conditions. We do this by moving the entire carton tray with its containers of seedlings to the porch for a few days where they are in a light shade and somewhat protected from the low night temperatures. Members of the cabbage family can be gradually hardened off to the point where they can withstand light late spring frosts. Tomatoes and other heat lovers like peppers can never be adapted to cool temperatures in this manner, however.

Take a look at your seedlings. There are two general growing types, so to speak. Some plants form a rosette of leaves low on the ground with the growing point deep in the center. An example would be lettuce. Others elongate with the growing point ever higher above the ground—broccoli is an example of this. Of course, some of the latter have weak stems characteristic of vines and grow out laterally along the ground unless staked or otherwise propped up—for instance, cucumbers and some tomatoes and squashes—but for purposes of transplanting this variation doesn't matter. The important thing is: avoid getting the growing point covered with soil or mulch.

This means careful planning in setting out the low-growing types because you want their centers to be slightly higher than the level of the bed. Achieve this by planting them in a tiny hill or mound with a depression around it to hold water. The long type of seedling, on the other hand, can actually be planted deeper than it stood in its first container. Tomatoes particularly will benefit from this treatment and will produce extra roots along the sides of the stem where it is buried. This type of seedling must also have a depression around it to hold water. When you move the seedlings, do so very gently. Remember, the water-absorbing rootlets are only one cell large and very fragile. If they are damaged, the seedlings' ability to take in water and minerals will be temporarily reduced.

Moving the seedlings out of the milk cartons is simple. When the cube container is lifted out of the tray and set on the ground, a slight wiggling of the paper sides will allow you to lift the carton shell right off, leaving a perfect cube behind with a seedling in each corner.

Now, with two hands, break the cube in half, and then in quarters. Each quarter can then be slipped into the ground wherever you desire. If you cover your beds with a thick mulch, as we do, the surface of the ground will be very soft and crumbly. All you will need to do is pull back the mulch and the top half-inch or so of soil with your fingers, set the little seedling down in the slight depression you've created, pull the mulch back around the cube of soil and press it down very firmly all around so that the roots make a good contact with the soil. Then water.

If you have made a slight depression around the seedling with the pressure of your hands, the water will soak in right around the transplant instead of running off the bed. We have spoken before about the importance of not disturbing the soil when it is wet. If you use compost mulches as we do, you will be able to do your planting in the middle of a rainstorm since you never have to disturb the soil at all with this method.

After the water has soaked in, check to make sure no

mud or mulch has washed into the center growing point. If it has, remove it gently with your fingers or with a little twig so that the center will dry out.

If soil should fall away from the seedling as you are moving it from its original container, don't despair. Be sure to hold it by the leaves, *not* the roots, and plant it the same as suggested above, firming the soil well around it so the roots have good earth contact. When this does happen, or if you feel your handling of the seedling has been rough enough to destroy a number of the root hairs that absorb water, cover the seedling for a day or two with an over-turned flower pot. This is done to reduce water loss in transplanted seedlings.

When it is time to remove these flower pots, we do not take them away entirely, but rather leave them setting upside down in between the seedlings for a while. This reduces air movement over the beds and also discourages our cats from digging in the soft earth and destroying the young seedlings, as they dearly love to do. These over-turned flower pots also provide a habitat for a number of beneficial insects—more about that later.

It is wise to consider weather conditions when transplanting seedlings. They will dry out quickly on hot windy days. Early evening is often a good time to set them out. In any case, if possible keep those you're transplanting in the shade of your body and the ones waiting to be planted out of the hot sun too.

If you suspect the seedlings are about to wilt, either because of rough handling or the heat of the day, it is wise to remove at least one big leaf to reduce water loss. Pinch it off with your thumb and fingernails. If the plant is already quite large and wilting badly, take off more than one leaf. As long as you leave one leaf and do not harm the center growing point, the plant will survive. As a matter of fact, our guess is that more transplantings are lost because their sentimental owners felt it was too cruel to cut them

back, than have ever been harmed by being pruned too
severely!

Transplanting Trees:
An Aside

While we are talking about transplanting, let us point out
that the most popular way to kill transplanted trees in our
area is by setting them in a depression so that water collects around the trunk. Fruit trees particularly, but many
other trees also, are susceptible to a variety of plant-
disease-causing fungi that can attack right through the bark
where the trunk joins the main roots, if that area is allowed to remain damp.

Usually a hole is dug first, then the tree seedling set in so
that the point where the main roots diverge from the trunk
appears to be at the same level or sometimes slightly
deeper than the ground around the hole. Then the soil is
packed in around the tree, leaving a depression which is
promptly watered and which fills with water every time it
rains or the area is sprinkled. What happens is that the
newly fluffed-up soil in the hole begins to subside, settling
the tree down even deeper. Furthermore, ground water
from the surrounding soil may tend to flow into the somewhat more porous earth in the hole. The end result is ideal
for the growth of pathogenic, or disease-producing, fungi.

What you should do: plant your tree seedling so that the
point where the main roots join the trunk is at least several
inches *above* the surrounding soil level. The earth should
slant away from the trunk so that water will drain off the
soil immediately adjacent to it. Then locate a ditch for
water *outside* that immediate area. A tree can only absorb
water through its smallest feeder roots and these tend to
be out near the edge of the leaf canopy under what is
called the drip line. So watering or fertilizing closer to the

trunk will not be of much benefit in any case, and excessive moisture there is likely to cause you to lose the tree.

Garlic Cloves, Tubers, and Other Possibilities

Occasionally you may wish to propagate plants vegetatively, rather than with seeds. When you take a piece of the plant itself and replant it, you have an exact duplication of the genetic material of the mother plant. With seeds, the offspring often exhibits some genetic variation from the parent plant as new combinations of characteristics may occur when the seed is fertilized.

Of the vegetables that the urban gardener is likely to be dealing with, potatoes, Jerusalem artichokes, garlic, leeks, onions, asparagus, rhubarb, and horseradish are all usually propagated by planting a piece of tuber, bulblet, or root of the plant.

Perhaps easiest are those where you simply separate the clump of bulblets and plant each separately. Garlic and shallots are the most common example. Set each clove in the ground so that the pointed end just reaches ground level. Leeks will also form bulblets around the mother stalk when it goes to seed. Separate and plant in the same way. In our mild winter climates, we have a saying, "Plant on the shortest day, harvest on the longest." In colder climates it will have to be either in late fall and covered with a thick mulch, or in early spring.

Some leeks will also form little bulblets in their flower heads, as will some onions, sometimes called multiplier onions. These can be broken off and planted, just like bulbs that form at the roots. Onions can be bought as "sets" rather than seed. These are little onion bulbs all ready to grow. Since it takes a long season to mature a bulb onion, this is a fairly foolproof method which provides a headstart. Onions form their bulbs in response to day length. Find out from your local agricultural extension people the best varieties for your area.

Jerusalem artichokes can be planted whole, or just a few left where they were grown, but potatoes should be cut, rather than planted whole, to produce good yields. Select firm tubers and cut the pieces so that each contains one undamaged "eye" or bud. Then let the cut surfaces dry for at least twenty-four hours before planting. We set ours out on top of the ground in the early spring and cover with a loose straw mulch. As the tuber begins to form, we reach in and detach them without disturbing the plant which goes on producing more.

Rhubarb, asparagus, and horseradish roots can all be bought through seed catalogs and all thrive best in deep loose soil with lots of organic material. Asparagus is a very satisfying crop if you have the permanent space for it. You cannot harvest it the first two years because the shoots you eat are the plant itself. They are needed to grow up, produce food, and develop vigorous roots so that the plant can stand cropping in future years. From the third year on you can harvest for six or more weeks in the spring, snapping the roots off at ground level with your fingers. The rest of the year, shoots are left to grow up and produce high feathery foliage which is a delight to view and is like the feathery, fern-like foliage frequently included with florists' roses.

chapter 9

Making Friends with the Neighbors, or Adventures with Chickens, Rabbits, Bees, and Worms

One way to become acquainted with the neighbors is to raise a rooster that crows at four in the morning (and every five minutes after that for several hours). You might think that delightful sound would produce sentimental reveries about our lost rural past. Not so. What it may produce is an irate phone call, "Get rid of that _____ rooster," and a knock on the door by the local police.

What are the laws in your community regarding the keeping of livestock within the city limits? In our town chickens are legal if they are kept more than twenty-five feet from the neighbor's residence, and even goats are permitted. But whatever the statutes in your community read, there is only one true law: *Don't annoy the neighbors!* It is only when someone complains that you will get into trouble, and then it won't really matter if you are obeying the letter of the law or not.

This means the urban gardener must give particular attention to animal noises and smells. The following descriptions of our various animal systems are written with these problems in mind.

Chickens or Manure, Eggs and Thoughts, by Bill

Neither of us can remember which came first, the chickens or the vegetables. We think the way it happened was: first we put in the plants, then we realized the great value of and need for compost. Next we discovered a need for a steady, reliable source of nitrogen for the compost. So we used to go down to the racing stables and beg them to let us in to get some of the manure. We would sort through the piles of discarded bedding until we located a catch of nuggets. "I found some," Helga would holler excitedly, holding up a batch of the treasure. "Pure gold," I would shout back appreciatively, and all the stablehands would give us peculiar looks.

My father told me the way to pick a true woman was to take her out to the stables and see if she would collect

feed trough

manure with you. Helga passed the test without a doubt. I had found a real woman, but we still hadn't solved our nitrogen problem. Going to the stables required gasoline expenditures, begging from usually hostile or unfriendly people (I wear a beard and that frequently sets the stage without a spoken word), and it turns out after all that horse manure is not very high in nitrogen. The solution was chickens which provide ample supplies, and this chapter is about some lessons well learned that would be of use to others who want to solve their fertilizer problems and get eggs and meat along the way.

Since deciding to get chickens, we've had some experiences with two different basic ways to keep the cackling fowl: in individual cages on wire and in a group on the ground with a coop. In order to help you decide which kind of system to start with, we'll discuss both, indicating advantages and disadvantages. First, the wire floor method.

Having the Birds on Wire

The cages we used were once commercial cages sold as a unit with six compartments, sliding doors, and a slanted floor for the eggs to roll down to the front where they could be easily collected. We got ours by driving out to a chicken-producing area and calling around until we found a man who had extra cages. We paid five dollars back in '69. With this system, a trough is mounted along the front of the unit so each bird has access to feed. A water trough is similarly mounted on the back. Since we were interested in harvesting the manure, arrangements were made for it to accumulate beneath the cages for regular removal, using a small hand shovel (actually an old-fashioned coal shovel) and a bucket. For ease of removal about a one-foot space between the cage and the floor should be provided. The manure removal system is probably the most important part of any of these animal systems, because how the manure is managed will influence the fly population, and this

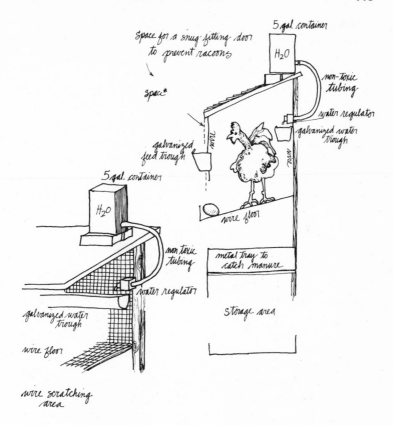

in turn can affect the neighbors and even public authorities.

The secret ingredient needed for all plant and animal life is nitrogen, and the best animal source, other than man, is chickens because 6 percent of their fecal material is nitrogen. Horse or cow manure, in comparison, doesn't go over 2 percent because their urine is seldom collectible. Chickens, on the contrary, have both fecal and urinary tracts combined, which explains why their nitrogen content is higher. Flies already know this secret, and you will have to manage the nitrogen sources to show people that you are responsible members of the community.

A useful point to help your case along is the fact that the major source of flies in urban areas is garbage cans. Some studies, where traps for the larvae (which are the young or feeding stages of flies—between the egg and pupa or cocoon—also called maggots) were placed beneath garbage cans to capture the larvae as they migrated out of the cans looking for dryer areas to change to the fly stage, showed that about 1,000 flies per can every week were produced. Multiplying this number by the number of such cans in any particular area will indicate that a tremendous population of flies exists in urban areas. If you keep chickens,

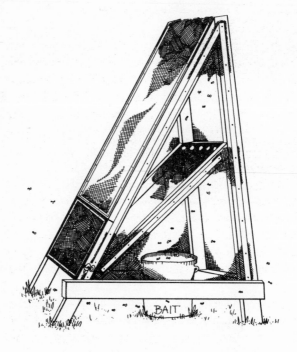

BAIT

*fly trap made from hardware
mesh and scrap lumber*

you will become aware of flies because even a well-managed system will still emit a little ammonia which will attract the adult flies. It would be a good idea to obtain a fly trap (Chapiewsky's Inc., Bangor, Wisconsin 54614, sells a good one). The catches make excellent chicken feed!

A most important way to manage flies besides trapping is to release certain beneficial insects that attack the flies in the pupal stage by boring in and eating the flies out. The insects can be obtained by writing Rincon Vitova Insectaries, Inc., P.O. Box 95, Oakview, California 93022. A shipment of fly parasites every month in hot weather at about three to five dollars per shipment would help provide a major reduction in the fly population.

The last important way to keep flies to a minimum is to manage the manure according to a regular schedule of removal and compost making. The most important thing to remember about manure removal is to leave a good portion of it to provide habitat and food sources for the beneficial parasitic and predatious insects already living in the manure. Just the other day I saw a beautiful new scarab (dung) beetle that I've never seen before. Lots of rove beetles also call dung "home."

The combined system of trapping, releases of beneficial insects, manure removal, and composting will easily keep any fly population under control and will surely pass the scrutiny of any official that may drop by to have a look. By carefully explaining your purpose and techniques you may even convince him that home food raising is the only way to go.

The wire cage method is best for manure harvesting, ease of egg removal, and reducing feed losses. Disadvantages include more maintenance, greater chances of lice because the birds do not have a chance to "wash" in the dust, and less entertainment possibilities since you miss seeing the pecking order and other shenanigans of a flock on the ground. The "on wire" system has enough disadvantages that, depending upon circumstances, we would probably recommend building a system where the birds are on the ground.

Having the Birds on the Ground

This system allows the birds to walk around a great deal more, hence they are usually tougher when placed in the pressure cooker after their egg-laying days are over. Still, they taste better than store-bought birds, have no hormones or other concoctions commercial producers are forced into using, and they take less care. The on-wire method we used meant someone had to go out and open and close the chickens each day.

This task, probably ominous at first, is not really that bad. I actually timed myself and could in two minutes in the morning feed and water both the rabbits and chickens. People watching this activity probably thought, "I wonder what that crazy man is doing now, jogging around the house." Of course, I'd have to run to do it in two minutes, but walking is permitted if you want to use a little more time. It's probably better on your own system to learn to go slower (but think faster). It's easy to lapse off into philosophy. I guess it's really a matter of not doing what the neighbors are doing but inwardly knowing that they will come around when they see your fun and success, especially after a few crises (like food and gas).

The basic idea with the on-the-ground system is to only collect the eggs each day and provide feed and water about once a week. This requires different kinds of feeders and waterers. We bought both of ours from Sears (which you can do through the catalog) for about five dollars each. Both could probably be made from five-gallon cans. A small coop should be provided for shelter in rainy and cold weather. Three to five birds per nest box is adequate. Smart systems we have seen and tested with a student project have a movable outside door that allows you to check the nests even while birds are sitting on the eggs. Oh yes, watch out about giving your eggs to young city kids; they actually try sitting on them, and, contrary to the success of the mother hen, they do not hatch into chicks.

Two other things are useful to know about if you use this method. One is litter management, the other is raccoons. Having the birds on the ground means they will have access to their droppings. Thus, whatever fly breeding occurs will shortly be controlled by the birds themselves, if there are no small areas inaccessible to the birds where manure will pile up. For the urban food producer interested in harvesting manure, creating a roost (where the birds can congregate at night) over an area that can be shoveled will probably provide enough nitrogen for composting. This way, a coop with roost, nest box, and a small walking, scratching area with the feed and water containers—all designed for ease of maintenance and harvesting manure and eggs—can easily be fit into the smallest backyard or rooftop.

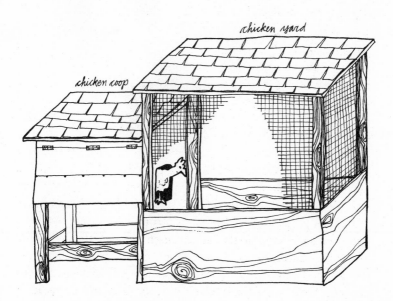

Raccoons like to kill chickens. For this reason adequate structures should be created. On wire the coop should be closed during dark hours to prevent contact between raccoons and chickens. On the ground, burying some of the chicken wire beneath the soil out to about a foot can prevent the raccoons from digging under the edge of the cage. All of our little hints that we are passing on to you cost us something—this one about the raccoons cost us seven brand new layers (it takes six months of feed to get the first eggs). If we have saved you even one problem, this book would be worthwhile.

Feeds and Foods

Before actually installing your birds, you need to consider feeds, their sources and composition. Feeds can be bought commercially, or the ingredients bought, then mixed yourself. Possibly feed can be produced completely at home (more about this later). Commercial feeds can be purchased at a feed store or a pet store. When you start it is probably best to get "complete mash" (usually sold by the pound or in 100-pound sacks) which will be good for both developing chicks, laying hens, or even meat chickens, but is usually more expensive. Possibly, if adequate pest-free storage space is available, you can get two kinds of feeds, the complete mash and a "laying mash" for the layers. Meat chickens can be fed scraps and many things which the others cannot because their requirements are not so delicate.

You can begin mixing your own feed by first shifting away from complete mash to a mixture like 1/3 complete mash, 1/3 recleaned wheat, and 1/3 fine cracked corn. A similar mixture is 1/4 each of complete mash, wheat, corn, and scratch. If your feed source (look in the phone book) sells them in fifty-pound bags, make batches of 150 pounds up and store it in a large (thirty-two gallon) plastic garbage can; the best ones have metal handles that snap over the lid. We keep ours on the back porch. Avoid spilling any feed, as it brings mice around. Once mixed, feed can be easily metered to the chickens. Using the first mixture, one of our students has determined that it takes about 25 cents per day to feed eight layers who give us six or seven eggs. If a dozen eggs costs 80 cents, you can easily see a savings, without considering the value of the bird and manure and without changing the feed in any way.

If you are willing to experiment a little, you can easily cut into the feed costs. The first experiment is to locate a good clean source of fresh grass clippings. Chickens will eat up to 1/3 of their diet in grass or greens. Chickens will eat lots of other things too, including insects, snails and slugs, dog food, and other foods. With the help of our students, we have embarked on a program to discover how much of their feed can be produced right here in the city. The directions we are exploring involve producing eatable foods from various cultures set up for that purpose. Earthworm cultures are a good example. Others which we have planned to explore include snails and slugs, sowbugs, crickets, flies, midges, and other insects. I should stress that flies can be trapped very simply and are gobbled up by our birds. We will soon evaluate how much of the diet can be made up of other organisms that can be easily and cheaply raised.

Before discussing selecting breeds and rearing chicks, two last bits of information about feeding chickens are important. All chickens need small stones, or grit, fed in their food. These really act as chicken teeth, for they are used to grind up the grains. They can be purchased, sifted from stony soils, or picked up when chickens forage. The other important feed ingredient critical for egg production is a supply of calcium. We use oyster shells and crushed egg shells. The former can be purchased while the latter can be collected in the kitchen. If you collect the egg shells, be sure to keep using them up quickly because some small residue of the eggs remains when you remove the ingredients and it starts to decompose after a week or so. Even if you use egg shells, some source of calcium should be added periodically to keep egg production up. I cannot see why lime cannot be added to the feed.

Selecting Breeds

Breeds can be selected for egg production, meat, or show, depending on your purpose. We have studied at least three different breeds in our systems: White Leghorns, Reds (Rhode Island and New Hampshire), and Plymouth Rocks. White Leghorns are usually chosen by the large grower for egg production. They start to lay early (twenty to twenty-four weeks) and lay up to 300 eggs per year. However, for the home grower they are a bit too fierce and nervous. The Plymouth Rocks are smaller birds with more meat, very calm and adaptable, but lay fewer eggs. The Reds appear best for all-around qualities: they lay well, up to 250 eggs per year, are large and meaty enough to make a good meal, and are relatively adaptable. New Hampshire Reds appear easy to obtain. Sears sells them, but local breeders can usually be found in most areas. If you want the more exotic breeds, wish to experiment, or merely want to look at a nice catalog, try writing to Murry McMurry Hatchery, Webster City, Iowa 50595.

Baby Chicks

If you get a chance to buy chicks that you pick out yourself, check their feet, bills, and vent (combination anus, vagina, urethra, and egg passageway) for abnormalities. Pick vigorous, healthy looking birds and see if you can get all females if you want only egg layers. You can mail order (usually along with another grower) only females if you want to pay extra. If you get both sexes, you can raise the roosters to eating size and bring them to the plate before they crow so that you don't annoy sensitive neighbors. You should leave one rooster to fertilize your eggs in order to raise chickens from eggs, but you do not need a rooster to get eggs. We recommend a flock without a rooster for crowded urbanites so as to avoid losing the flock altogether due to an unhappy neighbor.

Before obtaining the chicks, however, it is best to set up their living quarters. We have explored both wire and on-

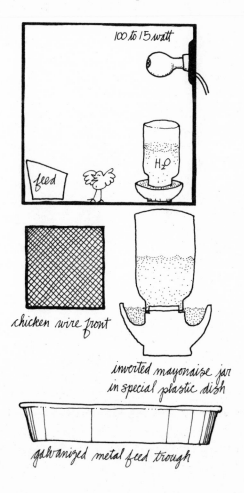

100 to 15 watt

feed

H₂O

chicken wire front

inverted mayonaise jar
in special plastic dish

galvanized metal feed trough

the-floor systems just as with the larger birds. We recommend an on-the-floor system that is at least a foot high, with a sawdust floor and a waterer and feeder bought at pet or feed shops. The waterer should be elevated so as to minimize fecal contamination of the drinking water. We use a sawdust litter to catch and dry the feces, and we change it about every one to two weeks, depending upon the number of birds and their age. The neat metal tray with head holes to allow the chicks access to the food without scratching in it is probably ideal because it reduces feed losses.

The last thing needed is a source of heat. We built our incubator from an old box, and installed a light socket inside it. When we first get the chicks, we use a 100-watt bulb and gradually over about a six-week period reduce the wattage to fifteen. Then it's outside to a cage with a light for similar adaptation and then into the final cage.

We have new chicks around our house about every month and they are a delight to watch grow. We have an incubator set up in the living room where we can peek in and enjoy the action. Since we have no television, it provides a source of entertainment when we are weary of the hurried world.

Other Details

Even though I'm approaching raising chicks in a "how to solve or go around the problems" way, do not think chickens are all problems. They are a delight to be near and really give your home a big survival advantage. Then again, much has already been written about how to do it all, but most of the literature requires interpreting since it has usually been researched for the large or commercial producer without considering the special circumstances of the small-scale home producer, much less the urbanite.

A good example is the one-sheet answer published by the

University of California Agricultural Extension Service, called "Precision Debeaking of Week-Old Chicks." The sheet tells how to use a debeaking machine. Debeaking is a process designed to just take the points of a chicken bill off so as to prevent them from killing or otherwise damaging each other. The fact that the chickens actually will kill certain members of their flock may have to be experienced to be understood. Since chickens peck each other in order to establish a social order in which the head chicken pecks the most and gets pecked the least, if their bills are pointed, a wound will frequently be opened. Once blood has been exposed, they all start to peck at the poor thing, and before long a dead chicken will result. But rest assured that debeaking will reduce the losses from pecking.

Now if you could simply get a bit of information about how to do it with a pen knife or razor blade, it would be nice. Since I know of nowhere to get it, I'll make it up for you. The whole trick is to cut the beak as you cut your own nails: cut the excess without cutting any living tissue. The skin part of the beak should be avoided. For people who have never done it before, try a little bit first. It's good to start on an older bird, but best to do it on younger birds about a week old. My complaint about the extension service's information is that it's all mostly geared to the big farmers and not the home producer. Keep this in mind when you read all information about food production. It will provide a good approach to interpreting a lot of useful research.

Harvesting

Usually it is important to inform people who have never grown their own food before that death is necessary if there is to be life. Killing a chicken humanely and quickly can result in a deeper appreciation of life. It is also surprising how many people do not know how to accomplish the task of taking a bird to the plate. My own views on the subject lead me to muse on how little real knowledge exists in a modern industrialized society with its compartmentalized functions. People, it seems, know how to reproduce, eat, make war, and die, but miss the joys of growing their food. The harvest of a chicken is a time when I also think of the day I too will join the earth.

The process for killing a chicken, plucking and dressing it, is a series of techniques that has been our pleasure to teach to hundreds of people. Before we die, perhaps thousands more will relearn a dying art.

After starting a large kettle of water boiling and after selecting the bird (usually a young rooster), I take it to a location where I can hang it upside down by its feet. It is best to restrain the wings because they frequently flap after the animal has been killed. By holding the neck down with the left-hand thumb under the beak and the rest of the hand behind the head, the neck can be stretched down. With a deep slice of a sharp knife, the large veins in the neck can be severed. Be sure to push the knife to the spinal column. The bird will die quickly, and the blood collected in sawdust is valuable as a source of nitrogen.

After a short waiting period, the bird can be dunked into boiling water for 1½ to 2 minutes to loosen the skin, lifted for drip draining, and placed on a cutting board for plucking. With two people plucking, the feathers can be easily removed in fifteen minutes, and the bird is ready to clean, cook, and eat.

Meat Rabbits

The ideal meat animals for urban areas are rabbits.

Compared to chickens, rabbits are quieter, less expensive to raise, and provide something chickens can't: fur or skin. Chickens require grains which humans could eat directly, but rabbits can be largely raised on market scraps or green plants produced in the backyard. We easily raised a litter on alfalfa, harvested from a plot approximately ten by twenty feet, to prove it to ourselves. (This was in the student garden where we could devote that much space to alfalfa.) The meat that rabbits provide is extremely low in fat. Chickens, including their eggs, are well known for fat content, particularly cholesterol. Rabbits are likeable because they respond to contact (petting). Of course, if you can have both, do so, but if you have to start with just one type of animal start with rabbits; it will be easier.

Hutches

We learned a great deal about adapting a rabbit system to a crowded urban area. Our first hutch, for instance, built largely from wood, was great for about two years and then problems started. The problems concerned the taboo area in the American psyche: wastes. The steady exposure of urine on wood creates a smell. This is how we met our neighbor on the north side of the house. A bachelor, he complained that the smell drifted into his windows when he was entertaining. Because of a lack of room beneath the wire floor, the manure built up to unacceptable levels. This combination of problems forced us to consider other housing. Today's hutches have evolved a great deal from the "ole" days.

The disadvantages of the first design were eliminated by using all-wire cages surrounded by urine guards, suspended about ten inches above deep, eight- to nine-inch metal manure pans with open ends for easy access with a shovel. The urine guards are particularly important. These are wide strips of sheet metal attached to the cage so as to cover the first five inches around the base of the cage and hang down about five inches. These guards prevent the wooden hutch structures from becoming contaminated with urine. By positioning the hutch close to the compost bins, the problems of moving the manure any great distance can be reduced.

If you make your own wire cages be sure to get strong wire and build them with sturdy fasteners. We recently bought special wire clips and clinchers from the Crown Iron Works Company (1205 Central Ave., N.E., Minneapolis, Minnesota 55413). It is definitely a sad thing to wake up one morning to find your hutches torn apart and your rabbits dead from a dog attack. The best way to prevent such occurrences is to build a dog-proof cage. Other predatory animals should also be built out. A friend of ours had trouble with a large gopher snake which dis-

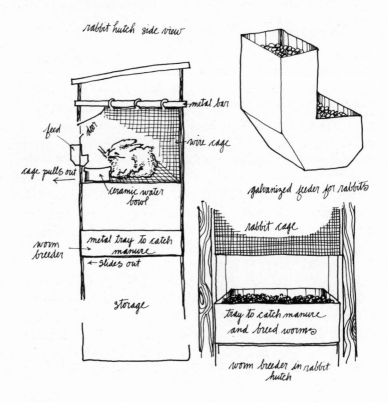

rabbit hutch side view

feed
door
metal bar
wire cage
cage pulls out
ceramic water bowl

worm breeder
metal tray to catch manure
slides out
storage

galvanized feeder for rabbits

rabbit cage

tray to catch manure and breed worms

worm breeder in rabbit hutch

covered that baby rabbits were tasty snacks. No greater than one-half-inch wire spaces will probably be enough to screen out such visitors.

The size of the cage is important. Our decision was to allow a greater area for movement than is normally allotted in a commercial situation. The commercial cages we obtained (very cheaply) were thirty inches wide, seventy-two inches long, and eighteen inches high. This cage was divided into four compartments, with presumably one rabbit per compartment. Anything larger would certainly be an improvement in living for the rabbits. Since the rabbits are to be placed in one's body eventually, it is important to understand that the better the rabbits are treated, the better one ultimately treats oneself.

Feeders and Waterers

When we started we made our own. We chose ¼-inch plywood and made the proportions to fit the rabbits. We learned a lot from this experiment and not just how high a rabbit's chin was. The feeder was also built so we could fill it up and let the rabbits eat; we thought this would reduce the time needed for frequent feedings. The whole thing turned out to be a disaster. We learned that it is bad to provide food continuously. Overfed rabbits get fat. Fat rabbits are not healthy and besides it is a waste of feed. We also learned that rabbits like to eat wood. It was easy for them to take some alfalfa pellets, then a bite of the feeder, then some more alfalfa, etc. The result was a holey feeder. Holey feeders don't hold feed.

We learned another thing about feeders besides not to make them of wood. If the feeders are placed so the pellets are accessible to the rabbits but can be loaded from the outside, time can be saved. This and more still we learned when Bill discovered fabricated sheet metal feeders at a local feed store. The price was right, and he tra-la-la-ed home and mounted them from the outside. Hurrah for some technology! Some humans before us had already made the same discovery. We had not done our research but now we appreciate what it takes to pioneer.

Our latest feeder discovery concerns what are called "fines." Fines are the small particles of alfalfa that build up in the feeder. When they build up to a considerable pile, some smart aleck rabbit decides to dig out the food dish, resulting in loss of feed. One day while looking through *Countryside Small Stock Journal* (subscriptions are available from Rt. 1, Box 239, Waterloo, Wisconsin 53594) we saw feeders with wire screen bottoms. The idea behind these devices is easy enough to figure out so we went outside with hammer and nail and fixed all the feeders to let the fines through. No feed loss now, except the fines.

Many Antioch College/West students helped us with these projects. One student suggested we build mangers so that the rabbits could be fed greens without opening the cages. The mangers also keep the greens off the floor of the cage; once rabbits start to walk on their food they often lose interest in eating it.

Waterers went through a similar evolution. We started with the galvanized sheet metal ones that Bill fabricated, which leaked. We turned to aluminum and even plastic but these needed to be tied down to resist being dumped, chewed, or otherwise destroyed. The solution was at the local feed store: ceramic bowls. We did learn one winter that frozen ceramic water bowls crack, but they can be glued back together. Only one of about ten bowls decided to express itself in this way so the bowls should be useful in cold areas too. Fill the bowls with a watering can.

Bill can feed and water the rabbits in less than two minutes if he rushes, but it takes longer to feed them fresh greens and pet each one. More realistically, five to ten minutes a day to feed and water and about one hour a week for cleaning, repair, and butchering could provide one's family with a cheap and friendly meat supply that produces fertilizer for the garden and leather for clothing. Obviously we like rabbits and rabbit meat. Before you can consider how to accomplish getting the bunnies to the plate, you should first get some bunnies.

Buying and Sexing

Some people give away their pet rabbits while others sell them. Either way, check them out for obvious signs of bad health. Watch how they move around; look for jaw, limb, or other bone disfigurements; check out the ears and feet. If you have a choice, choose animals without ear sores (due to an ear mite) and without sores on the feet. Pet the prospect and feel how sturdy he or she is. Compare with other rabbits. Stunted rabbits, from improper feeding, are not healthy, and may have small litters.

Usually, when buying new rabbits to set up a home system, you will want at least two or three females and one male, and thus you will need to be able to tell the sexes apart. Being able to sex the rabbits can save you money and time because if you want three females and one male and get two females and two males, you will need another female ($) and need to butcher the extra male. Oh yes, the higher price you pay for a ready-to-breed female is related to the time and feed it took to get her to reproducing age (about six months).

Young rabbits are difficult to sex but after two or three months it is easier. First, however, you need to know how to hold and move the rabbits around. Basically there are two ways: 1) behind the neck or by holding and moving them by the scruff of the neck with one hand while the other supports the greater weight under the back—best for large rabbits; or 2) the "loin" grip: by the lower region with the heel of the hand toward the tail of the animal—

better for the smaller animals. Whatever the method, be careful. Rabbits can give you some good scratches.

Once you have handled a few rabbits both ways you are ready for the next step in the process. Starting with loin grip, lower the animal quickly and steadily to where its head can be held firmly between your knees. This should immobilize the rabbit's front legs leaving you with both hands to keep the hind legs from scratching you with one hand, while leaving the other hand free to inspect the genitals. By blowing on the fur around the genitals you can begin to see where you can press gently to expose the penis which is contained in a tubular sheath. Obviously no penis means a female, but sometimes with young animals it is difficult to distinguish the protruding vaginal area from an immature male organ. A little experience always helps to clear up the muddle. The technique can be quickly learned and is important.

We should add here a bit about the educational value of learning and showing others the skills associated with raising rabbits. Not only are the "facts of life" easy to illustrate but nutrition, health and disease, the wonders of nature, confronting death, and other complexities all can be easily understood, learned, taught, and discussed through raising rabbits, or for that matter by caring for any form of living being. Once you appreciate such things it is also easy to see how far urban-suburban people have gone away from "the good life."

Breeding

Rabbits are notorious for their quick and easy breeding capabilities. Here is our technique for telling when a successful mating has been accomplished.

When the male mounts the female and goes through the motions of insemination, that mating is usually successful if, at the end, the male's bottom tucks under the female's and he flops over on the side. When you first start breeding, see if you can observe this. Most books recommend that three to five days later the male be placed back in with the female (always move the male to the female or move both to neutral or new quarters) to see if she refuses the male. If she does, she is pregnant and will drop her young between the thirtieth and thirty-third day, counting from the successful mating.

Once you know a female is pregnant, make a note on the calendar to put a nest box in on the twenty-seventh day. Earlier, the female will use the box as a defecation station, but if too late she will have her young on the floor of the cage where they usually die from exposure and lack of care (rabbits will not, like cats, carry their young around). You can tell a female is ready to drop when she starts pulling hair from her body and making a nest.

Another important point to keep in mind with pregnant or new mothers: they are extremely skittish or nervous during the gestation period, and if disturbed by noises, animals, food changes, etc., they may respond by eating their young. However, usually with a little care, having rabbits is like falling off a log. A burlap sack hung over the front of the cage may provide seclusion for a new, or about-to-be, mother if your yard gets a lot of visitors.

Feeding

Feeding is easy. One rule will do: don't overfeed. The way we learned this was to try different schedules and amounts, then compare the size of the fat deposits at slaughter time. Too much fat means a waste of feed and unhealthy rabbits. When we teach people how to kill and butcher a rabbit we always point this out. The lesson takes a while to learn sometimes, because we all like to eat and rabbits are no exception. For a full grown "California" breed rabbit, five ounces of alfalfa pellets each day is plenty. This amount can be decreased if greens are given. In cold weather they may need more feed.

Feed can be purchased, obtained as waste products, or produced. Alfalfa pellets are available at pet and feed stores in fifty and 100 pound sacks. Growing your own feed alfalfa is best, if you have the space. You can raise rabbits all the way with alfalfa except during the first weeks when they need mother's milk.

The supermarkets and grocery stores throw all sorts of greens and vegetable scraps away. While shopping, you can bring home a box or regularly stop by, make friends, and get such goodies as carrot tops, outer leaves of lettuce, cabbage, celery, etc. In fact, you can experiment and bring home salads with parsley, onions, radishes, etc.

Other waste products that you can start experimenting with are ornamental plants. Grass clippings are readily available, nutritious, and usually thrown away. Be careful about your sources, though, because lawns are heavily treated with herbicides, fungicides, and insecticides. Check about this first, and look further if the people look at you oddly. But if you explain that you want the grass for rabbit feed (chickens also love it), you may have a convert on your hands, especially in these times of high meat prices.

Over the last few years we've been trying various other ornamentals as foods and you can do likewise. Fresh leaves and twigs of many shade and fruit trees are gobbled up. It's a good game to learn which ones they like or don't like. They love linden leaves, but eucalyptus, pines, and acacia are largely refused. They eat bamboo and ivy.

A few common weeds and ornamentals are poisonous. A book called *Poisonous Plants of the United States* by Walter Muenscher (Macmillan, 1962) may be useful to you. The University of California Agricultural Extension Service has published a useful list of poisonous ornamentals. Why bother to learn which wild and ornamental plants in your area are good for feeding rabbits? Because not only is it cheaper to feed them on things others throw away, but also you become less dependent on materials that must be trucked into the city from somewhere else.

Other plants that we eat have also turned out to be good rabbit foods. Besides the obvious vegetables, we've fed them Jerusalem artichokes, miner's lettuce, and nasturtiums, all of which we have plenty of since they are almost like weeds. *Fresh* water must always be available.

Rabbits can stand very cold weather if they are kept dry and draft-free. But they are sensitive to heat. If your summer temperatures go above 95°F regularly, then avoid breeding the rabbits during this time and locate their cages in a shady spot. During real heat waves, a fine spray of water over the cages, or wet burlap cloths hung over the wire, will help reduce the heat stress they may suffer from. We prefer to breed and butcher our rabbits in the winter, although our town has a rather cool summer, because the pelts are so much thicker when it's cold.

Butchering

There's lots more to learn about the furry little chewers, but to start you off right, you need to know how to get the rabbits from the hutch to the plate. The steps in the process are slaughter, butchering, packaging, storage, preparation, and eating.

The best, cleanest, and easiest way to render a rabbit unconscious is by dislocating its neck, or by stunning it with a sharp blow at the base of the skull. An excellent description comes from Farmers Bulletin No. 2131, called *Raising Rabbits* (it can be purchased for less than twenty-five cents by writing the Superintendent of Documents, U.S. Government Printing Office, Washington, D.C. 20402).

"To dislocate the neck, hold the animal by its hind legs

with the left hand. Place the thumb of the right hand on the neck just back of the ears and place the fingers under the chin. Stretch the animal quickly by pushing down on the neck with the right hand. Press down with the thumb, then raise the animal's head with a quick movement to dislocate the neck." This method is instantaneous and painless when done correctly. I always make sure by using a stout stick to crack the skull.

Suspend the carcass by inserting a hook between the tendon and bone of the right leg. Insert the hook just above the hock. Cut into the skin just below the hock of the suspended leg, then slit open the skin on the inside of the leg to the base of the tail. Continue the incision to the hock of the left leg. Separate the edges of the skin from the carcass and pull the skin down over the animal. Leave as much fat on the carcass as possible. Remove the head, cut off the tail, the front feet, and the free rear leg at the hock joint.

After skinning, make a slit along the median line of the belly. Remove the entrails and gall bladder, but leave the

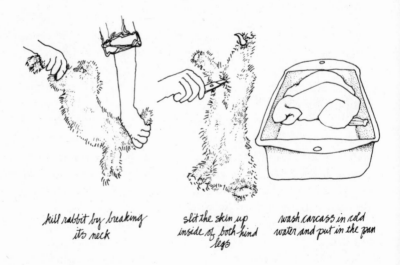

kill rabbit by breaking its neck

slit the skin up inside of both hind legs

wash carcass in cold water and put in the pan

liver and kidneys in place. Be careful to avoid spilling the bladder contents on the meat. Unhook the suspended rabbit and remove the right hind leg at the hock.

Wash the carcass in cold water. Chill the carcass in a refrigerated cooler.

An excellent pictorial description of dressing or butchering a rabbit is contained in the 4-H Club Rabbit Project Manual (4-H-Ag51) and can be obtained by writing to Cooperative Extension Service, College of Agriculture, University of California, Berkeley, California. Essentially the rabbit is hung upside down by the hind legs, skinned, dressed (much like a chicken), cut into various portions—ribs, legs, and back—to be used in different dishes, packed so as not to push holes in a plastic bag, labeled, and put into the freezer for preparation at a later date—or eaten that night for supper.

Most of the recipe books that mention rabbit at all usually say to prepare it like chicken. This is generally true, but actually a still greater variety is available because portions of the back can be ground into rabbit burgers or sliced into small pieces for incorporation into many Chinese dishes. There is also rabbit stew, sweet and sour rabbit, and many others.

Tanning

A friend of ours, Les Auerbach, who lived with us for a while, taught us how to tan our rabbit skins. This is the method he uses very successfully:

1. Take care of the skin when it is first removed from the animal—slip it over a hanger and let it dry in a cool, shady place. Leather should *always* be kept out of the sun! Originally we immediately salted the skins heavily, but more recently, having read a government booklet that says one should never do so, we have just let them dry as they

came from the animal. Since rabbit skins are so small, it seems desirable to accumulate several before beginning the tanning process, and then do them up all at one time.

2. When you are ready to begin the process, cut the pelts through one hind leg so that they will lay out flat.

3. Soak the skins in a bucket of cold water for about six hours. Les would do six pelts at a time, thus the recipe here is for that number. Keep the pelts submerged under the water with a brick.

4. Remove skins from water and "flesh." This means pulling off the thin membrane and any clinging fat that might adhere to the inside of the skin. This is done with a sharp skinning or jack knife, usually holding the skin over the edge of a board. How well the skin comes out at the end of the process depends on how thoroughly and skillfully the fleshing is done. It does take experience, as the skins are thin and it is all too easy to poke through the pelt accidentally. It used to take Les about fifteen to twenty minutes to do each skin, but if you've never fleshed a pelt before, allow more time in the beginning.

5. As soon as each pelt is fleshed, return it to the cold water. Do not leave the pelts exposed to the air any longer than you can help it.

6. Make the tanning solution. Commercial tanning companies have a variety of formulas, usually kept secret, and many contain caustic chemicals. The solution Les used contains materials fairly easy to obtain.

For 6 rabbit pelts:

> 1 pound of potassium alum, dissolved in 1 gallon of cold water.
>
> 8 ounces of salt, and 4 ounces of washing soda, dissolved together in 1/2 gallon of water.

Important—first put alum solution in a plastic barrel, porcelain crock, or glass container. Do not use metal. Then, add soda-salt solution to alum water.

7. Put wet, fleshed pelts into a container of the tanning solution. Les used to emphasize that soaking, fleshing, and putting in the tanning solution all should be done in quick succession.

8. Leave in tanning solution for four to seven days. Keep the container in a cool, shaded place.

9. Stir the tanning pelts at least twice a day. Keep them submerged in solution at all times.

10. After four to seven days, remove pelts and rinse thoroughly in cold water. Les recommended doing this several times.

11. In the next to last rinse, use one ounce of borax for every one gallon of water and leave skins in water for about five minutes, agitating them occasionally.

12. Give them a final rinse in plain cold water.

13. Squeeze out excess water from the pelts, gently. Do *not* wring—treat as you would a fine woolen garment.

14. Stretch on a board to full size, fur side down, and pin down the edges with thumb tacks.

15. Rub a bar of Ivory soap into the skin side, working up a good, thick lather with the moisture that remains in the skin.

16. Let dry in a cool, shaded place. This may take from one to several days, depending on the weather.

17. When thoroughly dry, you can rub in a little neat's foot oil, and work the skin back and forth between your hands, if you wish them to be very soft. This step is not absolutely necessary. If you get oil on the fur side, clean with cornmeal.

18. Sew into garments, either fur or skin side out, depending on your desire. Mittens, vests, and bed spreads are all good possibilities for these useful, pretty little skins. Ten to twelve skins, from medium-sized rabbits, will make a man's large, warm, wind- and drizzle-proof vest.

Excellent booklets on the entire process, including garment making, can be obtained from Mr. and Mrs. Devereaux, 724 N. Verlinda Ave., Lansing, Michigan 48915.

Sources of Information

Rabbits

American Rabbit Breeders Association, Inc., 4323 Murray Ave., Pittsburgh, Pennsylvania 15217, publishes a basic guide book which is an excellent source of information. Available with membership, $5/year (as of 1974).

Countryside Small Stock Journal. Rt. 1, Box 239, Waterloo, Wisconsin 53594. Usually has something about rabbits, also good advertisements for supplies. $5/year (as of 1974).

Domestic Rabbits, official publication of American Rabbit Breeders Association, Inc., had its first issue January, 1973. Good for the larger breeder. A few dollars/year. Write Bill Dorn Associates, Inc., 5350 W. 78 Street, Minneapolis, Minnesota 55435.

Meck, M. W. *Rabbit Raising For Profit*. New York: Greenberg Publisher, 1947, 356 pp. Loaded with all sorts of good stuff not available elsewhere, including recipes, anatomy, parasitology, genetics, and how to process angora wool. Meck also wrote about eight other books you may be able to find in used book stores.

Templeton, G. S. *Domestic Rabbit Production*. Danville, Illinois: The Interstate Printers and Publishers, Inc., 1968, 213 pp. An excellent all-purpose book for the rabbit raiser, but still geared to the commercial rabbitry. The book costs about $6.

U.S.D.A. *Selecting and Raising Rabbits*. U.S. Agricultural Information Bulletin No. 358, 1972, Superintendent of Documents, Washington, D.C. 20402. 15¢. The pictures are especially good.

Bees

Bees were probably the earliest domesticated animals. The process of first raiding a wild hive and then learning to move the hive, say in an old tree trunk, when the tribe moved seems to be what may have occurred when man followed wild herds in their migrations, or when he sought new lands after the older areas filled up with people. Whatever the origin, bees can provide both sugar and protein, the two major food sources which sustain the body.

Most people know bees can produce honey and that was our reason to start raising them. Our first hive was installed in the teaching garden we and our students created in the middle of Berkeley. The ulterior motive behind setting up the hive was to demonstrate that a sugar source could be created close to major concentrations of people that would require no pesticides and antibiotics to support. This could then offer an alternative to the system required to make the white sugar most people eat. If you actually look behind the scenes of sugar beet production, you will find that great amounts of herbicides, fungicides, and insecticides, besides large expenditures of fossil fuels, are used to produce white sugar. Even if you are suspicious about the value of this white sugar and have heard stories about its contribution to tooth decay and ill health, knowing what it takes to produce sugar from the sugar beet could leave a bad taste in your mouth.

It is, however, a long way from this bad taste to developing a wholesome sugar source. This chapter is a look backward at our adventure with the busy bees and some hints about how to adapt them to city life.

Our first bees were a gift from a fellow entomologist, Dr. Dudley Pinnock, who was studying the diseases of bees at the University of California. He gave us a docile strain that was not a heavy producer but still gave enough honey to make keeping them worthwhile.

Bees are social insects and many people become fascinated with the parallels between human communities and insect societies. Some direct parallels include the hive and house, guard bees and soldiers, and nurses and teachers. Within a colony the actual tasks performed by workers could be construed by some to be beauticians, masons, cooks and bakers, pathfinders, and even morticians. One author goes a step further in using analogies to describe a colony of social insects; he thinks the parallels between the social insect colony and the human body are remarkably close. In his view, the workers and soldiers are the blood cells of the body—the workers being the red blood cells that do the major work while the white blood cells are the soldiers that keep out invaders. The queen is the equivalent of the brain and the sex cells, and the sperm and egg in the human species find their equals in the nuptial flight when the many males or drones mate with the queen.

All analogies break down eventually, and the actual wonder of bees should be appreciated directly. A healthy hive can contain up to 50,000 workers, and during the peak honey harvesting season, as many as 1,000 workers die every day. The queen, being the principal source of new workers, is busy replacing them. She can lay in excess of 1,000 eggs per day, and can live for many years. Workers, also females, have traded the monotony of only laying eggs for a diverse but much shorter life. The basis of this trade-off may even be the secret of the hive. It is instructive to follow the life of a bee starting from when the egg is laid.

The queen starts the process by parking her elongated abdomen down into a cell and depositing a whitish egg on the bottom. Three days later the egg hatches and the developing grub or larva starts to be fed by nurse bees. For the first three days of their lives, all bees are fed royal jelly. Only the queen is fed this richer food for her entire life. Royal jelly, also called brood food, is a protein-rich secretion from the glands of certain, mainly young, worker bees.

If the workers stop feeding royal jelly, the larva will turn into a fellow worker. Once this change has occurred, no special diet added later will turn the developing bees into a queen. For the next five or six days the workers-to-be are fed a mixture of honey and pollen. After this feeding period, the larvae are sealed in their cells by wax caps placed over the cell by workers. Each larva spins a cocoon and changes into a pupa. During the pupal stage, larval organs are replaced by adult-like organs—a most remarkable process.

Twenty-one days after being deposited by the queen, a young bee chews her way out of her cell. She looks wet and bedraggled but soon tidies herself up and begins to beg food from older sisters. She also takes pollen which helps her to produce royal jelly which she will soon yield. Her first few days are occupied in cleaning out cells and keeping the brood warm.

From about the third to sixth days she feeds older larvae. After that her glands produce the royal jelly which is fed to the young larvae and queen. About two weeks later she starts secreting wax from abdominal glands which is used to build the cells and comb. Soon after this she starts making a few play flights to familiarize herself with the hive surroundings. Then she becomes a forager who collects nectar and pollen, guards the hive, collects water, and accomplishes the chores of the hive.

She also collects propolis, a sticky resinous substance obtained from many sources—poplar buds, resin from pine trees, and elsewhere. This is used for sealing cracks and gaps in the hive. The California Indians learned to use this substance to waterproof their baskets.

After we installed our bees, it was all Bill could do to take his eyes off them. He just sat for a long while and watched them landing and heading into the dark interior of the hive. Others would walk out of the darkness and fly out of sight. By sitting next to a hive and watching this action, you can learn to move slowly and tune in on their hum. You will also notice that certain numbers of incoming bees will have whitish or yellowish balls attached to their rear legs. These are pollen balls, gathered from flowers to be fed to larvae. Pollen is a rich source of protein which can be harvested, actually stolen from the bees as honey is, by building a pollen trap that forces the incoming bees to pass through small spaces that knock the pollen off their hind legs. Good beekeepers know how much pollen to take without setting the hive back too much.

Bee lore—business, hobby, and biology—is large, deep, and important in the lives of us all, though few people realize it. Most urbanites fear bees as they fear most insects. By having and learning how to keep a hive, you can obtain a source of food and a source of pleasure for a lifetime. Some of the literature at the end of this chapter could be useful if you are interested in pursuing some of these ideas further.

An Ant-Proof Hive Stand

Beehives and human homes both are subject to invasions by various species of ants. Exclusion as a management strategy can work effectively in both cases. In homes, the technique is to trace ant columns back to points of entry and plug the holes permanently with putty or other crack sealers. The idea is to force the ants to go greater distances for their food until the food energy harvested is not worth the energy expended to obtain it. Repeated efforts using this approach result in permanent alteration to the home environment. A similar approach with beehives can save the continual efforts and costs necessary to poison ants, contaminating the environment in the process. This is a story about how an ant-free and pesticide-free beehive was developed.

Over the last 100 years the Argentine ant appears to have taken advantage of man's methods of moving materials around the globe. Originally native to South America, it is now known on every continent but Asia, and even there it may be discovered or will occur once widespread trade opens with China. In California the species is best known because of its house-invading habits and because it protects many honeydew-producing insects (e.g., aphids, scales, mealybugs, whiteflies, etc.).

In Berkeley the insect is virtually ubiquitous—in the garden the ant was everywhere! This at first was disturbing. Its numbers were extremely high, and we, like most others, had our share of insect fear (entomophobia). After time and much observation the ant became regarded as beneficial because of its role as a soil aerator and mixer, as a scavenger, and an insect predator. Where the ant was a problem, i.e., with aphids and other honeydew producers, a band of Stickem®, a sticky nontoxic material (available from Michel and Pelton, Emeryville, California), applied to the plant stems excluded them. Where such an application was excessively time consuming, a high-pressure stream of water directed at the aphids reduced the population below damage levels.

When a few ants were observed trying to get into the hive through the entrance, we studied the situation. Apparently guard bees were occupied in buzzing the unwelcome guests away. This activity went on for weeks without a successful invasion. Bill thought then that the widespread use of various pesticides (e.g., chlordane, arsenic, and mirex) had no foundation. An observation one day changed his mind. One afternoon, about two years ago in the spring, during honey flow (this is a term which indicates peak honey production), he passed by the bees and noticed to his surprise that the entire hive was literally covered with ants, all three supers! (Supers, in case you don't know, are the wooden boxes that make up the hive.) The bees were obviously upset. Their hum was intense and flight activity around the hive excessive, even for that time of year. The ants were streaming in the entrance and had found another opening where the cover had warped. The bees had formed a concentrated mass at one side of the entrance and were frantically buzzing ants away from their side. Swarming seemed to be their next move. Bill quickly began an attack to save the hive.

He began by running his hands over the masses of ants on the outside of the hive, crushing hundreds with each pass. Remembering that the ants disliked water, he called someone to quickly bring the hose. With the hose he began to soak the area around the base of the platform upon which the hive rested. Then he saw that the ants were avoiding the water and swarming from subterranean areas onto the mat of morning glory vines under and around the base of the platform. Bill quickly weeded around the hive, throwing the ant-covered vegetation away. This and the water now had stopped the major ant access to the hive. The hum of the hive and circling bees dropped perceptibly. About ten minutes had passed, but it seemed like an hour.

Obviously the bees liked the help, but more still had to be done. Now with the help of a student, who was directed to crush the ants on the outside of the hive, we removed the cover. Inside the ants had virtual control of the top super. Only sporadic worker bees were interacting with one small group of ants. Occasionally a bee would move to the top edge of the super, interact with an ant or two, and fly off. One bee flew off with an ant locked to its leg by the jaws. Each frame was systematically removed and the ants eliminated one by one. On one frame a queen ant was discovered coming out of an empty, partially filled honey cell. Possibly the ants were making ready to set up a colony in the hive. This seems probable since the species is known to reproduce colonies by budding, where one of its many queens moves off with a group of workers and sets up house. Throughout this careful mopping up activity, the hum of the bees continued dropping, the potential swarm disappeared, and foraging activity returned to normal. A total time lapse of about thirty to forty minutes had occurred.

With a sense of relief and new-found respect for the ant, we removed ants from ourselves, rested, and began planning a protective device for the hive. After a brief search for materials, a crude hive stand was fashioned using wooden legs and oil-filled milk cartons. A student volunteered to evaluate this first stand. In the next few days an unacceptable number of bees were being killed and otherwise damaged by landings and explorations in the oil containers. Another stand was made without oil but with Stickem barriers. This was effective for months until

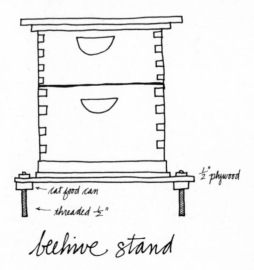

$\frac{1}{2}''$ plywood

← cat food can

← threaded $\frac{1}{2}''$

beehive stand

weeds, dust, and water made the barrier passable. Another design incorporated upside down cat food cans with Stickem on the inside walls protected from rain and dust. To everyone's consternation this design also proved ineffective when the weight and excessive leg height (about one foot) combined to topple the hive. Today's hive stand has six-inch-long by one-half-inch threaded steel rods.

Throughout this adventure, as the stand evolved we first sought to develop a nontoxic method that worked. This stand is our best effort to date. At this stage, the cost per hive appears prohibitive for large commercial operations but feasible for the hobbyist or other small-scale producers who want their own honey. However, if pesticide costs increase because of shortages of raw materials, such stands may become widespread. In the future we hope to develop other hive stands.

Speculations about similar adaptations for human habitats suggest a construction technique to exclude ants from homes without using insecticides, while simultaneously leaving ants to prey on other insects and fill their niche as decomposers and scavengers.

Bees and Diseases

Little honey produced in this country is poison free. Most beekeepers that make a significant portion of their income from bees, which means hundreds and sometimes thousands of hives, use antibiotics to suppress particular bee diseases. Reading the literature about these problems appears most foreboding. It also seems that legally a beekeeper is required to report his hive(s) to local authorities and county agricultural officers. The trouble starts when your hive is inspected. Although our hive was never inspected, some beekeepers indicate that subtle and other pressures are brought to bear which force people to begin using antibiotics as a preventive treatment.

First, using antibiotics routinely as a preventive, without any sign or warning of disease, will lead toward destroying the antibiotic tool because resistance will develop and then it will be no help. Second, because the beekeepers dust the hive with the antibiotic, it means the honey produced is laced with the stuff. Since we eat the honey, we also eat the antibiotics. Of course, we are all assured that the amount we eat has not been shown to be detrimental. But from our viewpoint, it is a bad idea to eat antibiotics, especially ones that are also used to treat humans. For example, one of the common bee antibiotics is Terramycin which is also used in managing human ailments. This is important because if one needs an antibiotic but has been ingesting it for some time in honey, there is a possibility that resistance to the antibiotic has already developed, and it will be of no use. Multiply this by millions of cases, and you get to understand the scope of such a problem.

From the standpoint of an urban gardener who wants to manage his or her hive(s) without antibiotics, it will probably take more knowledge, attention, work, and cost because you will have to do it all yourself. First, you will need to read up on the diseases and learn how to recognize them (see literature at end of chapter), and then learn how to treat for each without resorting to an antibiotic. To do all this, you will probably need to like bees and learn about their lives in detail. Start there, then maybe find a beekeeper who can tell you how he does it, or find a teacher who can start you off right. Correspondence courses are very inexpensive (see end of chapter). Agricultural extension people are easy to connect up with, and bee societies can be contacted. Writing experts is also possible. Starting at a library is a good idea. Our approach to learning anything is twofold: "the idea side" and "the do side." The approaches for the idea side concern thinking, reading, writing, and listening. The approaches for the do side involve learning the actual tasks. We jump into projects, planning to learn on the way. Our advice to others usually is a mixture of both important ideas and how to start. We hope this is what we've given you with this chapter.

There are some precautions you can take to avoid stings from bees, wasps, and hornets, when you are outside where these insects are most populous:

Don't wear perfumed material, such as hair spray, suntan oils, after-shave lotion, etc.

Wear white or very light clothing rather than bright colors.

Walk around, rather than through, wild and other flower masses.

Avoid areas where food and cooking odors are attracting wasps, such as outdoor barbecues and open refuse containers.

On picnics, take a chunk of meat (chicken, tuna, or liver are good) and set it off to the side. This will serve to attract wasps away from the picnic table. Wasps also like highly sugared liquids such as soft drinks and sweet juices (especially Hawaiian Punch).

If you are extremely sensitive to wasp or hornet stings consider having yourself immunized rather than dousing your entire area with insecticides. (Remember the story of the king who was so delighted with the feel of leather under his bare feet, he ordered the entire country paved with leather from border to border. Whereupon a wise man suggested he tie a piece of leather under each of his feet to achieve the same effect!)

Immunization has proved very successful in helping allergic people. "Progression to more serious reactions was halted for over 97 percent of treated persons and, in most instances, responses were noticeably lessened or reduced to that of a normal person." This information comes from the Allergy Foundation of America, 801 Second Avenue, New York, New York 10017. You can contact them for literature and general information on desensitizing treatments for insect stings.

Sources of Information

Bees

Books for Beginners:

Dadant, C. P. *First Lessons in Beekeeping*. Hamilton, Illinois: American Bee Journal, 1947.

Eckert, J. E. and F. R. Shaw. *Beekeeping*. New York: The Macmillan Company, 1960.

Free, J. B. *Insect Pollination of Crops*. New York: Academic Press Inc., 1970.

Grout, Roy A. *The Hive and the Honey Bee*. Hamilton, Illinois: Dadant and Sons, 1963.

Kelley, Walter T. *How to Keep Bees and Sell Honey*. Clarkson, Kentucky: Walter T. Kelley Company, 1941.

Morse, Roger A. *The Complete Guide to Beekeeping*. New York: E. P. Dutton and Company, 1971.

Root, A. I. *ABC and XYZ of Bee Culture*. Medina, Ohio: The A. I. Root Company, 1962.

Other Valuable Books:

Andrewes, Sir Christopher. *The Lives of Wasps and Bees*. New York: American Elsevier Publishing Company, Inc., 1971.

Beekeeping in the United States. Agriculture Handbook No. 335. U.S.D.A., Washington, D.C., U.S. Government Printing Office, Superintendent of Documents, Washington, D.C. 20402

Insects. U.S.D.A. Yearbook, 1952. U.S.D.A., Washington, D.C., U.S. Government Printing Office, Superintendent of Documents, Washington, D.C. 20402

Laidlaw, H. and J. E. Eckert. *Queen Rearing*. Los Angeles and Berkeley: University of California Press, 1962.

Lindauer, Martin. *Communication Among Social Insects*.

Cambridge, Massachusetts: Harvard University Press, 1961.

Maeterlinck, M. *Life of the Bee*. New York: New American Library, 1954.

Pellett, Frank C. *American Honey Plants*. Hamilton, Illinois: American Bee Journal, 1930.

Phillips, Mary. *The Makers of Honey*. New York: Children's Book, Crowell Company, 1956.

Ribbands, C. R. *The Behavior and Social Life of the Honey Bee*. Bee Research Association, New York: Dover Publications, 1964.

Seeds. U.S.D.A. Yearbook 1961. U.S.D.A., Washington, D.C., U.S. Government Printing Office, Superintendent of Documents, Washington, D.C. 20402

Snodgrass, R. F. *Anatomy of the Honey Bee*. Ithaca, New York: Comstock Publishing Associates (a division of Cornell University Press), 1956.

Von Frisch, K. *Bees: Their Vision, Chemical Senses, and Language*. Ithaca, New York: Cornell University Press, 1956.

Von Frisch, K. *The Dancing Bees*. New York: Harcourt Brace and Company.

Pamphlets:

Fundamentals of California Beekeeping, Manual 42, Calif. Agr. Ext. Service, $1.00.

Pennsylvania Beekeeping, Circular 544, Pennsylvania State University, College of Agricultural Extension Service, University Park, Pennsylvania, free or inexpensive.

The extension service in your area will probably have similar booklets.

Correspondence Courses:

Pennsylvania State University

Entomology 70. Beekeeping. The course gives the life history and habits of the honeybee, methods for successful production of comb and extracted honey, seasonal management, rearing of queens, control of bee diseases and enemies of the honeybees, preparing comb or extracted honey for market, and marketing methods. 10 lessons, 8 study points. Revised 1971 by W. W. Clarke. Write to: Correspondence Courses, The Pennsylvania State University, 307 Agricultural Administration Building, University Park, Pennsylvania 16802.

University of Minnesota

Entomology 0-004C. Principles of Beekeeping. Useful to the nonexperienced and experienced beekeeper. History of beekeeping, life history and behavior of honeybees; colony and apiary management; pollination and hive products; honeybee diseases and their control. 16 lessons, 3 certificate credits. Basil Furgala, Associate Professor of Entomology. Write to: Department of Independent Study, University of Minnesota, Minneapolis, Minnesota 55455.

University of Missouri

Entomology 109. Beekeeping. This course covers the entire field of beekeeping. It includes a study of such practical work as hiving swarms, moving bees, extracting honey, packing bees for the winter, rearing queens, and the like. It also covers the more technical questions of external and internal anatomy, brood rearing reproduction, and the like. One or more colonies of bees should be available for use with the practical work. 2 semester credits. Write to: Independent Study Department, Extension Division, Whitten Hall, University of Missouri, Columbia, Missouri 65201.

Cornell University

Home Study Course in Beekeeping. This course answers the need of New York beekeepers and beekeeping hobbyists for information and training that will make their apiaries more profitable. An apiary is not necessary since the course does not require actual handling of bees. Persons who sell apiary products as a sideline will profit by the suggestions made through this course, based on successful practices of other bee-keepers. 9 lessons, 3 practical exercises. Certificate of course completion. Dr. Roger Morse. Write to: Home Study Course in Beekeeping, Department of Entomology, Cornell University, Ithaca, New York 14850.

Ohio State University

Course No. XVI. Beekeeping. This course is a practical one, offering suggestions for the amateur of the "What," "When," and "How" of practical beekeeping. The lessons cover in a condensed way the whole process of bee management, under the following headings: Choosing the Apiary Site, The Organization of the Colony, Brood Diseases, Spring Management of the Apiary, Extracted and Comb Honey Production, Marketing of Honey, Fall and Winter Management of Bees, Rearing of Queens, Increasing the Colonies, and Honeybees for the Orchard. 12 lessons, revised 1965. Write to: Extension Specialist, Apiculture, The Ohio State University, 1735 Neil Avenue, Columbus, Ohio 43210.

Free from University of California Agricultural Extension Service (University Hall, U.C. Berkeley, California 94706):

Pollinating Alfalfa With Leaf-Cutting Bees	AXT-160
Honey Bees in Alfalfa Pollination	AXT-228
Toxicity of Pesticides and Other Agricultural Chemicals to Honey Bees—Field Study	AXT-251
Honey Bee Pollination in California	AXT-252
Why and How Honey Bees Should be Protected	AXT-268
Honey Bees in Almond Pollination	OSA-196
An Observation Bee Hive	OSA-108
Beehive—California Plan	OSA-217

Cantaloupe, Cucumber and Watermelon
   Pollination   OSA-231
Toxicity of Pesticides and Other Agri-
   cultural Chemicals to Honey Bees—
   Laboratory Study   M-16
An Economic Analysis of the California
   Bee Industry   MA-29
Journals and Societies:
   American Bee Journal, monthly, Hamilton, Illinois
   62341.
   Bee Research Association, a world bee research organiza-
   tion, publishes a journal, *Bee World*; an abstracting ser-
   vice, Apicultural Abstracts; a scientific journal; books;
   and pamphlets. For further details and membership,
   write Bee Research Association, Hill House, Chalfont
   St. Peter, Gerrards Cross, Bucks, England.
   Gleanings in Bee Culture, monthly, A. I. Root Co.,
   Medina, Ohio 44256.

Raising Earthworms

Why do we raise earthworms? To put into our garden
soil to improve it? No. The earthworms that can be raised
in manure, kitchen garbage, or compost are a different
species from those that live in the soil. They need a richer
medium in which to grow and reproduce, and will not
thrive in the quite different environment of your backyard.

Do we raise them to decompose our compost, improving
its plant nutrient qualities before it is added to our soil?
No. Each time food is passed through another animal,
some energy is lost. Just as you get more energy from a
given amount of corn or wheat when you eat it yourself,
compared to the amount of food you get by feeding it to a

chicken and then eating the meat, so also do you waste energy by passing your compost through earthworms before putting it out on the soil.

If you put the finished (cool) compost directly on the soil it will nourish the types of earthworms that naturally live there. These will then multiply and do their work of breaking down the compost material, incorporating it into the soil and creating good soil structure while they do so. However, if we didn't have the space or inclination to maintain a compost system we probably would use earthworms to decompose our kitchen wastes and rabbit manure.

Why do we raise earthworms, then? To feed chickens, fish, and other animals.

You will need:

1. Earthworms—the species called "manure" worms. They are frequently sold in bait shops or through magazine ads urging you to develop a business selling them.

2. A box, preferably at least eight inches or a foot deep. Fruit lug boxes work well and are easy to move.

3. Bedding material. Peat moss or sawdust is good. Torn paper strips can also be used.

4. Some organic material for the worms to eat. Rabbit manure and kitchen garbage are both excellent. You can also use compost.

5. Agricultural lime. Sprinkle a very small amount over the beds once a month or so, and water it in. This will prevent the cultures from becoming too acid.

Our most successful earthworm culture was started right in the manure pans under the rabbits on our roof. First we put down three inches of *thoroughly* dampened peat moss. Then we added the manure worms and gave them an inch covering of coarse compost. Soon the rabbit droppings provided all the food they needed. In the warm spring and summer temperatures they multiply rapidly. In cool weather (below 70°F) they will breed very slowly.

There is always a danger of the culture getting too dry, particularly on the roof where it is windy and hot. The rabbit urine provides some moisture, but we add additional water occasionally—usually just rinsing out the rabbits' water dishes over the beds takes care of it.

When you have plenty of big adult worms, you can start removing them for chicken feed. Put the culture, bedding and all, through the coarse screen to remove the large worms, always leaving some breeders to keep your culture going along.

chapter 10

Managing Wildlife
in the Urban Garden

Wildlife in the City

Our town stretches from the shores of the San Francisco Bay up to the top of the Berkeley hills. On the inland side of this rise lie many miles of regional parks. In even the most densely built part of the city it is not uncommon for deer from the parks to wander down into backyards. Deer can be pretty destructive. Many ornamental plants as well as vegetables suit their palate. Yet hardly anyone thinks of reaching for a rifle. Local camera club enthusiasts wait eagerly for a chance to catch them cropping the roses.

Raccoons are frequent visitors to many homes in town. In spite of the danger of dogs, entire families of them—mama, papa, with babies in tow—can be seen climbing along the fence tops in the late spring and summer when the cherry plums are ripe. Out of the first batch of hens we raised from chicks, seven were wiped out in one evening by raccoons—their necks wrung. We felt terrible. Our response was to build strong doors to cover the chickens at night, and we haven't lost one since.

Then our egg production went down. We couldn't understand it. One day Bill went out to close the chickens up a little later than usual and, in the beam of his flashlight, he caught sight of a young possum, his gleaming teeth cradling an egg. We borrowed two wildlife traps, the kind that drop a lid when an animal goes inside. After that, each morning we would go out to find one or the other of our cats in prison. "What I've got to put up with, living with you folks!" was the expression plainly written on the face

of our old tom. Finally, Bill managed to capture the possum in a fish net—we carried him off to a new home in the
country.

Birds come after the strawberries and other vegetables.
Friends of ours developed an ingenious chicken-wire enclo-
sure for their garden, approximately ten by fifteen feet,
with a mechanism to lift the roof effortlessly so that one
could step inside to plant, weed, or harvest. When our
cherry plums were disappearing we were ready to buy a
large nylon net to throw over the tree. Then we discovered
the culprits in jeans and sneakers.

Deer, raccoons, possums, birds—for most city dwellers it
is a thrill to be so close to wildlife. Unless the damage gets
intolerable, they delight in these visitors from the "natural
world." When the destruction becomes severe, they find
various mechanical or physical ways of dealing with it,
traps and barriers being first choice. But insects, ugh!
That's a different matter.

Entomophobia

People are afraid of insects and other creepy crawly
things. We've all been brought up on a diet of comic-book
insect monsters, movie and T.V. horror insects, with pesticide manufacturers and pest control operators doing their
bit to encourage this revulsion. No one looks at an insect
on a plant and asks, Is it doing intolerable damage? The
reaction is, see it, kill it.

Fear of insects and insect-like creatures is called entomophobia. Most humans in our culture share this to some
degree. Once, when Bill worked for the state public health
department, a woman called him up in hysterics about a
spider. "I've emptied the whole bug bomb on him and he's
still moving," she screamed. Spiders are very valuable in
controlling pest insects. Helga knows that now, but as a

child was irrationally afraid of them. A movie seen at an impressionable age, in which a little boy was bitten and made sick by a large tropical spider (the entire sequence a very Hollywood concoction), made an indelible impression.

Embarrassment over an incident in her teens (in which, in front of people whose respect she valued, she jumped up and screamed when a little grass spider ran over her leg) finally did it. A determined effort devoted to looking at and reading about spiders finally proved a cure.

Natural Controls

If two flies were to breed without restraint and all of their offspring to do so as well, their breeding potential would be so great that in a single summer they would cover the earth thousands of feet deep in flies. But this has never happened. Why not?

Many conditions control insect populations without any interference by man. Temperature is an obvious one and so is humidity. Different kinds of insects have different tolerances, but for any one population it can get too cold or hot, too wet or dry. Availability of food will affect population size. Squash bugs cannot live on ash trees nor ash bugs on squash plants. Endless acres of carrots or cabbage obviously can support larger populations of insects associated with those crops than a few specimens of the same plant in a planter box. The right habitat is essential for any animal. Overturned flower pots in our yard, though not originally put there for that purpose, have provided habitat for predacious ground beetles and spiders, both of which are welcome. Boards for walking on when the ground is muddy have encouraged the most unwelcome proliferation of slugs and snails, whose numbers appeared to be determined not only by food but by the shade the place offered during the day.

Availability of fertile mates is important, too. Certain insect populations in some areas have been reduced by purposely releasing sterilized males reared in the laboratory. Every female mating with a sterile rather than a fertile male will have lost the opportunity to give birth to another generation of her kind.

Another important aspect of natural controls is disease. Insects get sick, of course, just as other animals do. Finding a sick insect in the crop, mashing it up with water, and spraying the mixture around on the other insects to infect them with the same disease is a valuable biological control method which has led to the refinement and marketing of several commercially available products.

Perhaps best known, since it has been used in this country for the longest time (about 15 years), is a bacterial preparation of *Bacillus thuringiensis*, sold under trade names such as Biotrol,® Dipel,® and Thuricide,® and sometimes referred to as B.T.

Insect diseases tend to be specific to certain groups of insects (B.T., for instance, is effective in controlling only certain caterpillars). The insects, their diseases, and man have evolved over millions of years in the natural environment together; man has not been adversely affected, and the insects have not become resistant to the diseases (in contrast to many pesticides containing materials never present in biological systems before they were synthesized by man in the laboratory). Thus, insect diseases are a particularly effective and environmentally safe means of reducing the insect population.

Carnivorous Insects: Parasites and Predators

Among the most important controls on any herbivorous or plant-eating population are the carnivorous insects that feed upon them. These are parasites and predators. Parasites are usually quite "host specific"—that is, able to live in or on only one particular kind of insect or very restricted groups of insects. The little miniwasps which we work with that parasitize certain aphids are an example. Predatory insects are more easily recognized by most people, the best known and liked being ladybird beetles and lacewings.

One tends to think rather simplistically of these carnivorous insects as being the "good guys" and herbivorous plant-eating insects as being evil. It is good to remember that many plant-specific insects help to keep potentially serious weeds in check. By taking advantage of this knowledge some noxious weed invaders of range and waterways have been controlled by bringing in the insects that feed only upon them. St. John's-wort, prickly pear, puncture vine, and alligator weed are examples of such exotic weeds controlled by deliberately introduced specific herbivores.

Also, let us not forget the herbivorous silkworms and bees. Most people do not realize how dependent we are on these latter plant-feeding insects; some of them directly pollinate the crops we eat, and others are eaten by the animals that provide us with meat and milk. Beneficial insects have their parasites and predators, too, and in general it is safe to say that insects are very important in the natural control of other insects.

Another Look at Insecticides

When the modern insecticide era was ushered in with DDT during World War II, all us insect-fearing and insect-hating people thought a miracle had come. Just push the button and they fall over dead! Some of the older insecticides were really dangerous to people, for example, Paris green (arsenic) and nicotine sprays. DDT didn't seem to hurt people and other mammals at all. Hurray! We poured it all over ourselves and our planet. (As recently as 1972 it was still being used to routinely douse prisoners in the California prisons as a protection against lice—for all we know it is still being done.) Hurray, we were to end all diseases caused by insects, all damage to food and fiber. DDT was thought to be a panacea.

It has taken a very long time for the whole story to become clear. Not all is known and understood yet, and even where the facts are in, many people have too much at stake economically or in terms of status to admit they might have been wrong.

Three R's and an S

The first effect that began to emerge, regarding the use of DDT and related "miracle" insecticides, is called the "residue" problem.

The First R = Residue

When you spray an insect poison you cannot avoid hitting more than the target organism. What you are *really* spraying is an entire environment or ecosystem. Some but not all of the older poisons were derived from plants. Such poisons, or "botanicals," as they are called, can be rather quickly decomposed by microorganisms. The new materials, of which DDT was an example (other common members of this group still in use are chlordane, lindane, dieldrin, endrin—called chlorinated hydrocarbons), are *persistent*. They did not seem to cause mammals much problem, but they were soon seen to accumulate in body fat. Most important, they move up the food chain, or "biomagnify."

An example of biomagnification: you spray a tree and each leaf receives only a small dose of poison. The leaves fall and the earthworms work on them and each earthworm eats more than one leaf, so he gets a bigger dose. The birds feeding in that area each eat more than one earthworm, so they get even a bigger dose. The cat that patrols the yard and catches birds there may get enough of a dose to noticeably harm him. It may not kill him outright, but it may make him more susceptible to some disease organism, affect his reproductive system, or cause premature failure of some organ under other stresses to which he may be subject.

Damage and death due to pesticide poisoning of this sort have two characteristics that should be borne in mind: they may not show up for a long time, and the effects may be indirect, involving other stresses in the person or animals involved, such as poor nutrition, weight loss, exposure to other specific toxicants or agents of disease, etc.

As this problem with the first group of miracle insecticides became visible, they began to lose some of their charm. People read Rachel Carson's book, *Silent Spring*, and for the first time began to realize that global contamination caused inadvertently by man could destroy the planet for us.

Over the last few years a general switch began to another group of poisons which were less persistent in the environment: the organo-phosphates. But the organo-phosphates have the disadvantage that they are much more obviously and immediately toxic to humans and other mammals. An example would be parathion, a few drops of which on the skin can kill a man. (Malathion is a member of the group much used by city dwellers because it is not so obviously toxic, but it is still a poison.) Then farm workers began to get sick.

In California we have struggled for a number of years to

get legislation passed that would offer greater protection to the large numbers of poor farm laborers who must handle these materials and the plants on which they have been sprayed. Since many of these people cannot read or speak English fluently, we tried to get different colored containers to indicate different degrees of toxicity. Because the labels often fall off or become illegible we wanted the label to be stamped into the material of the container itself so that it became an integral part of it. Needless to say, all such changes failed to be passed, largely because of efforts by the pesticide company lobbyists.

Growers have resisted offering handwashing facilities to the workers or marking the fields that have been sprayed with these materials so that people will know it is not safe to enter. Even when pesticide containers appear empty they often still hold enough poison to harm people, animals, or water supplies. Yet they are commonly abandoned in a dump somewhere to rust away or are thrown by the roadside to threaten the curious or ignorant. We wanted to see them returned to the manufacturers to be decontaminated—after all, they originally devised and then made a profit on the materials. But the growers and pesticide companies either defeat or find ways to get around this kind of legislation.

As the disadvantages of this second group of pesticides became clear, a third group was developed—the carbamates. A common one is Sevin, which we have seen advertised in garden magazines as the "ecological" or "environmentally safe" insecticide. This supposedly refers to the fact that carbamates are not too persistent, are not thought to accumulate in food chains, and do not seem to be very toxic to humans.

However, several other serious problems relating to the use of insecticides have begun to be understood. We are taking the trouble to spell them out here because we believe that some of the homemade concoctions to control insects in the garden may be just as troublesome as the more toxic commercial products.

The Second R = Resurgence

"Resurgence" refers to the fact that some time after you use an insecticide you may find that your insects are back but now in higher numbers than before. Plant-eating insects, as we have mentioned before, have carnivorous or meat-eating insects that prey upon them. Unfortunately, the poisons are often more detrimental to the populations of those carnivorous insects than they are to the pests. How can this be?

For one thing, some materials are selectively toxic to the large family of insects to which many of these beneficial insects belong. Sevin, for instance, is particularly deadly to honeybees and possibly to other members of that insect

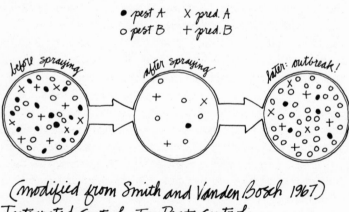

• pest A   X pred. A
o pest B   + pred. B

before spraying   after spraying   later: outbreak!

(modified from Smith and Vanden Bosch 1967)
Integrated Control. In Pest control:
biological, physical and selected chemical methods
ed. W.W. Kilgore and R.L. Doutt.
New York, Academic Press

family, such as the little miniwasps or parasites that control aphids, scales, caterpillars, and other pests.

Other reasons for these beneficial insects being selectively more damaged by the poisons have to do with their greater mobility and slower reproductive rates. They encounter more poison as they hunt around to find their prey, while a stationary aphid, perhaps protected by a leaf part, may avoid getting sprayed altogether. Besides, there are many fewer carnivores out there to begin with. It is rather similar to the situation with other animals. For example, you may have a large number of rabbits which reproduce themselves rather quickly and stay pretty close to home. These may be preyed on by just a few far-ranging coyotes that have only one litter a year.

The result of spraying poisons that kill the predators is that the prey population is left completely without controls. The few that survive the pesticide application, or those new pests that fly in from outside, are able to reproduce relatively unhampered by predation or parasitism. By constantly using poisons you may so reduce the natural controls on the pest insect that you need to keep spraying. You are caught on the "pesticide treadmill."

Lest you think that this disaster is caused only by commercial synthetic poisons, let me warn you that we have seen resurgence of pest insect populations, in this particular case aphids, by the excessive ill-timed use of water sprays alone. By knocking off, causing diseases in, or otherwise discouraging ladybird beetles, lacewings, spiders, and other important predators on these particular trees, the aphids remaining were able to resurge to even more damaging population numbers. We shuddered to read, in the letters-to-the-editor column of one garden magazine, of a lady who was spraying garlic on her plants every three weeks. No wonder she was having to do it repeatedly; she was probably indiscriminately causing all kinds of ecosystem disruptions. This would hardly lead to a stable situation.

S for "Secondary Pest Outbreak"

There is another problem related to this ability of pesticides to cause a resurgence of the pest, and this is called "secondary pest outbreak." The farmer, whether urban or rural, usually is only aware of those insects that are present in large numbers. He or she doesn't realize that every plant is the habitat for literally dozens of other kinds of insects besides the ones he calls pests. An alfalfa field, for instance, generally regarded as a monoculture, upon investigation yielded up a thousand different kinds of insects. The farmer was really only concerned with one or two.

Why are the other insects not noticed? Because their natural enemies, the carnivorous insects, are keeping them under control. Now what happens when insecticides (possibly even garlic sprays) are used? Some of the carnivorous insects controlling these other insects are killed off, releasing these potential pests from their controls. The result—entirely new bugs appear in great numbers and become a problem. These are called secondary pests.

In the San Francisco Bay area a local newspaper runs a gardening column written by an older gentleman who has highly respected horticultural skills. Alas, in his own garden, or so he claims in his column, he is constantly troubled with one insect plague after another for which he recommends poison after poison. Little does he realize that a goodly number of what he thinks are invasions of new insects are merely problems with bugs that were there all along and which he is responsible for making into secondary pests.

The Third R = Resistance

Another serious result of the exclusive reliance on pesticides on a world-wide scale is the problem of insect resistance. This is *not* similar to the situation in humans, when you build up an immunity to measles or some disease you've had before; it refers to selecting out a population for those individuals who already have an inborn ability to detoxify the poison. It is remarkable that these creatures who evolved on the earth before the development of man should have carried with them into the twentieth century the genetic ability to survive poisons that man has only recently dreamt up in the laboratory.

The genetic diversity of insects is so great that in every insect population that has been studied, besides those individuals that survive because they manage not to be in contact with the poison, some are exposed to it and yet survive to breed another day. Of course, when they do breed they find very little competition for food or habitat because most of the susceptible members of the population have been killed off. So, the more a poison is used, the more quickly an insect population becomes filled with individuals that are resistant to it.

This problem of insect resistance first became noticeable among the insects that were most vigorously attacked by modern insecticides, for example, mosquitoes that carry malaria, and the insects that eat cotton. In some areas of Texas and northern Mexico, cotton farmers drove themselves bankrupt by spraying so often that the bugs eventually became totally resistant and ate everything in sight. In California, where the mosquito control districts abandoned promising research on alternate ways of controlling these pests and turned to exclusively chemical controls, a serious condition now exists with resistant mosquitoes that carry encephalitis, a disease fatal to humans. Hopefully, funds will once more become available for more environmentally sound methods of controlling these insects. Some of this is already being supported in a small way through the laboratories at University of California at Berkeley where we work.

When we are out giving a talk on this subject we summarize all these insecticide-caused difficulties with the mnemonic: "3 R's and an S," which stands for Residue, Resurgence, Resistance, and Secondary pest outbreaks. Now that you are aware of these problems, doesn't it seem wise to reserve the use of all insecticides, even garlic or others that are relatively nontoxic to humans, for use only as a last resort, when the damage caused by the insect is intolerable, after you decide it is essential that the plant be maintained, and after trying all other techniques without effect? Even then there are *still* other methods.

What the City of Berkeley Did

One spring day several years ago, in the city of Berkeley, the truck was spraying pesticides on the linden trees as they had every year for many years previously. A young woman, Ms. G. Hilsman, who was gardening out in her side yard, saw the truck coming. She grabbed her child off the porch and, babe in arms, went out to halt it bodily. "Stop, I won't let you spray my organic garden!" Thus began the development of a pest management program for the city that has reduced costs as well as the use of pesticides.

Probably, if making a scene on the street was all that Ms. Hilsman was prepared to do, the city would have simply left her block alone and gone about their business as usual elsewhere. But she was determined to find a better way to manage the insect problems on the trees and she sought help from other interested individuals and groups through the Berkeley Ecology Center. There she was referred to a group of scientists and other citizens called The Northern California Committee for Environmental Information, which was in turn an affiliate of a national group called Scientists Institute for Public Information, the publishers of *Environment* magazine. We happened to be members of that group, interested in taking scientific information and making it generally available to the public. The most active members of their pesticide subcommittee were professors, researchers, and graduate students at the Division of Biological Control, U.C. Berkeley. It was a lucky connection for everyone concerned.

The city of Berkeley is generally extremely sensitive to citizen demands. Phone calls complaining about the excessive honeydew drip from the trees got them started spraying in the first place. Using pesticides was the only technique they knew about. With citizen encouragement, city officials in the Parks and Recreation Department made a cooperative agreement with the Division of Biological Control at U.C. Something new had definitely happened in the history of urban pest management!

Since the whole affair had started with the linden trees, this seemed to be a logical place to begin working on the problem of reducing pesticide use. People are nostalgic for the landscapes of their youth. The first settlers from the old country began immediate importation of plants to the new land, and pioneers moving west brought eastern species with them. The linden (*Tilia*) is a lovely shade tree, and the varieties usually planted in American cities were originally brought over from Europe.

As had happened many times, along with the plant came the herbivore, or plant-eating insect that fed upon it in its native land, but the parasites and predators of the insect were left behind. It is easy to see how this happens. The herbivore is stationary, often well disguised. Sometimes it may slip into the country in the egg stage when even careful inspection may not reveal it.

In the case of the linden, the accidentally imported herbivore was an aphid specific to that tree. In the absence of its natural controls it quickly grew to a population size of pest proportions. It is true that some native predators, which tend to be much less host-specific than parasites, did feed upon the newly introduced aphid. But with crucial components of its natural ecosystem missing, the aphid managed to keep way ahead of the less well-adapted local natural enemies.

The ironic part of the situation was that the aphids did not really seem to visibly harm the tree, although very high populations may have retarded its growth a little. (This may be a boon to some city maintenance personnel who use hormone growth regulators to avoid having to prune the trees.) The problem is that aphids, like scales, leafhoppers, and some other insects, produce a sticky excretion called honeydew. It is a high-protein sugar solution which is delicious to eat and from which an expensive honey is made that is sometimes available in specialty stores. Alas, this honeydew, if present in large amounts, may thoroughly coat the leaves of the trees and invite the growth of a black fungus called sooty mold, much like mold that sometimes grows on the sugar in a jelly jar. This mold seems not to harm the tree either; when the honeydew and mold are rubbed off, the leaf appears a healthy green beneath. But unfortunately, the honeydew may also fall from the tree like rain.

Beneath the trees are parked that all-American symbol of wealth, status, fertility, and sexuality—the automobile. That's where the trouble starts. People call city hall to complain that the tree is "sick" and they want to have the city cure it with some "medicine"—in this case a pesticide. We live in a society with absolute belief in the chemical cure. We also like our cars bright and shiny!

Dr. van den Bosch, chairman of the Division of Biological Control at U.C. Berkeley, remembered seeing linden trees in Rome and parts of France that had the natural enemies of the aphid. Supported by a small grant from the city, research was begun on bringing in the specific parasites that controlled the linden aphid (*Eucallpterus tilliae*) in Europe, in hopes that the cool Mediterranean climate of our town would be similar enough to allow the little mini-wasps to survive.

These little miniwasps are as tiny as their name implies and can be seen clearly only under a microscope. The one that Dr. van den Bosch went after, *Trioxy curvicaudus*, lives only on the linden aphid and has a very interesting way of life. The mother parasite inserts her eggs deep inside the living aphid. The miniwasp egg hatches into a little grub and begins to eat out the insides of its host, eventually killing the aphid and turning it into what entomologists call a "mummy"—a hard, shiny, round shell of an aphid with the living parasite inside. A careful look at any common aphid population, for instance, the one on cabbage, corn, or beans, will usually disclose the presence of several or more of these miniwasp mummies. But whether on the particular aphid population you happen to look at there will be a sufficient number of a well-adapted species of parasite is another matter. Many of these other pest aphids are also introduced from foreign countries and are thus without their natural enemies.

Inside the mummy the miniwasp pupates, or forms a cocoon, from which eventually emerges a full-grown adult. This, then, searches out another aphid in which to lay eggs and begins the cycle all over again.

These parasites never kill all the aphids in a population. As the number of aphids goes down it is harder for the parasites to find them, fewer parasite eggs are laid, and fewer parasites develop. As the parasite population goes down, fewer aphids are killed, and as the aphid population begins to expand there is more food for the parasites and their numbers also grow. And so it goes, neither eliminating the other, but each population keeping the other in control in a natural fashion, the way it has gone on in the wilds as long as these insects have been on earth. The

critical difference is that the aphid population attacked by
the parasite never gets as large as it did before the parasite
was established.

These miniwasps are so locked into the life cycle of their
aphid hosts that they cannot live on any other kind of
insect. Usually they cannot even live on other closely related groups of aphids! So you see, they are really the
"silver bullets" of pest management, since they control
only populations of a specific insect and do not harm anything else in the environment.

One must be very careful in introducing a beneficial insect not to bring in one that is not wanted. The truth is
that the food chain of these insects is even more complicated than we have mentioned so far. For in fact, these
little carnivorous insects that control the herbivorous
aphids also have carnivores that live on them. These are
often called secondary or hyper-parasites. It is not desirable to bring foreign hyper-parasites into this country. For
one thing, they may prevent a high mortality to the aphid
population; for another, they tend to be less host-specific
and may move over to other beneficial miniwasps as well.
Therefore all introductions are done very carefully, the
insects being passed through a strict quarantine procedure
which removes hyper-parasites, before being released in the
field.

This point in the story is where we came in on the scene.
We were also very concerned about pesticide use in the
city and Bill was looking for a good project on which to do
his PhD thesis. After all, we were growing our vegetables
here too. For the next three years, with the encouragement and assistance of the many entomologists at the lab,
and the intelligent cooperation of the city of Berkeley
parks and recreation personnel, we were able to reduce the
populations of the linden aphids as well as a couple of
other aphids, and best of all, institute a pest management
program for all the city trees. The biological control tech-

niques mentioned above are only one component of this overall program.

An Integrated Control Program

In every city where we have looked, we have found a situation that has led to unnecessary costs and undesirable pesticide use, namely, pesticides are used when there are no pest problems present. People spray by the calendar or because they've read or been told by pesticide company salesmen or other "advisors," that it's "that time of the year" to spray. This is similar to an organic gardener throwing around expensive rock powders, kelp meal, and such when their soils are not even deficient in those particular minerals, just because they read it in a book somewhere. Only, using pesticides unnecessarily is worse because they are poisons!

In Berkeley we asked the maintenance people to report all tree bug problems to us to inspect and advise on before they did anything—and not to do any "routine" spraying at all.

In other cases in other cities, we have found pesticides being used where there were high insect populations, but less toxic materials could be substituted for the sprays they were using. Water sprays have been used effectively in a number of situations; sometimes soap is added as a wetting agent. The important thing is to monitor the insect population and time the sprays so they will do the least damage when they are used.

On other occasions it was found that cultural or physical controls could be substituted for sprays. Sticky barriers were put around a number of trees to prevent ants (specifically the Argentine ant, *Iridomyrmex humilis*), which are attracted to the honeydew, from climbing up and protect-

ing the aphids by keeping away their predators and parasites. With other trees, pruning of the most affected areas
reduced the habitat favored by the insects, thus making
the problem manageable.

These techniques, all of which are useful to the backyard
gardener, helped to bring them down the pest management
costs to the city and eliminated the need for maintenance
people to handle dangerous materials.

In any case, a large part of a good integrated control
program should involve education. In a city this means
reaching the people who manage the plants as well as the
citizens. In your own home this means educating yourself
and your family. Insects don't exist in a vacuum. You need
to know about soils, climate, and good horticultural practices, as they all influence pest problems.

You have no doubt heard the myth that insects are less
likely to attack a healthy plant. That's nonsense. Insects
love healthy plants. Insects need good nutrition, too; in
fact, they will usually go after the healthiest part of the
plant, the young, vigorously growing buds and branchlets,
like aphids clustered on the end of a broccoli stem. What is
true, however, is that healthy plants can outgrow insect
damage more easily, as well as combat plant disease more
effectively.

Furthermore a complex, "healthy" environment that
provides food and habitat for a wide variety of insects will
also promote the development of insect parasites and predators that will help control pest insect populations. Flowers, for instance, provide nectar and pollen to feed some
beneficial insects. Mulches provide prey and habitat for
ground predators. A "wait and see" attitude towards an
insect population, where the "see" part means really observing what's happening, may be all that's needed to allow
the natural enemies of the insects to catch up with and
control them. Lots of populations are sprayed because
people don't know that the natural enemies always lag

behind their prey; many people cannot recognize the beneficial insects and are afraid to wait for natural controls.

Learn to recognize the wildlife in your garden and never kill an insect outdoors *just* because it is there! (Guess we'll modify that to—except mosquitoes!) What good is an aphid? It is necessary to keep the beneficial insects around, if for no other reason, so that the next aphid that flies into the area will find natural enemies ready and waiting.

A year ago, flushed with our success in the city of Berkeley, we vigorously attempted to interest other cities in supporting a similar program. We pointed out the considerable savings to the taxpayer, and the human health and environmental advantages of not using unnecessary poisons on city trees. After almost a year of trying to get such support, we are quite discouraged. We have talked to city governments, written popular articles, and published in scientific journals all over our part of California. Perhaps it will take a really large-scale citizen movement, or a great increase in the cost of pesticides, or both, before city governments will listen.

Biological Control in the Urban Garden

Two questions we are most often asked are: Should I import beneficial insects? What about companion planting?

Regarding the first, although bringing in beneficial insects has been a useful component of our integrated control program for cities, it is only rarely worthwhile for the home gardener. We would advise *against* importing the two predators most widely promoted for this purpose.

Ladybird beetles with winter fat deposits still in their bodies are often collected where they are hibernating in the mountains and sold to gardeners. Unless you mark the ones you release, as we did in a local experiment, you will not realize they fly away to burn off this fat before they can eat. Furthermore, so many beetles are killed in the process of collecting, storing, and shipping, that it is best to leave them alone to fly into your area of their own accord. These companies also help distribute the lady-beetle parasites, which could be very damaging in the long run.

Preying mantids are fascinating creatures and make good pets. However, importing them for pest management purposes is not advisable. They are only rarely able to survive outside of their native area. They are also totally unselective as predators, not discriminating between the beneficial insects and the pests.

Lacewings are beautiful insects that will remain in your area as larvae if they are introduced in the egg stage. They are general predators and feed on many pest insects. If you are interested in learning about beneficial insects, these might be good ones with which to begin. A twenty-minute color movie that shows the life cycle of the green lacewing and identifies many other important beneficial insects is called "Biological Control of Insect Pests" and can be rented from the University of California Extension Media Center, Berkeley, California 94720. It makes an absorbing and educational addition to a garden club meeting.

If you are keeping chickens in an enclosed area where their manure is allowed to pile up, you might be interested in importing miniwasps to control flies that may breed under such conditions. Both these parasites and lacewings are available from Rincon Vitova Insectaries, P.O. Box 95, Oakview, California 93022. They will send information on how to use the insects that you order.

Companion planting is another story. We've promised ourselves that in writing this book we would stick to the truth and nothing but—so we will have to come right out and say that all that stuff you've been reading about planting one plant to repel insects from another is about 95 percent or more wishful fancy. How come it is printed in so many places?

Authors copy from one another as well as truthfully report their own and others' real experiences. Unfortunately, just because you planted a certain plant and then found you either did not have a certain insect or didn't find it in the numbers that previously occurred doesn't really tell you what caused what.

You need carefully controlled experiments to find out if what you are doing is really having the effect you are observing. It is true, for instance, that marigolds give off a root exudate that will discourage nematodes. All nematodes? The answer is not known. There are more beneficial than harmful nematodes, in any case. How far away from the individual marigold plant will the effect reach? No one knows for sure. Are nematodes a problem in your soil? Many people worry about insect damage without correctly identifying the insects involved.

One man wrote us because he was worried about needing to fumigate his soils for wireworms, which he said were getting worse year after year in spite of his religious use of compost. When we asked for samples, what arrived were not wireworms (the larvae of a beetle) but millipedes, which generally function as harmless decomposers which eat dead and dying materials. Naturally one would have lots of them with the constant use of compost, and they are desirable.

It is said that mint keeps away ants. But which ants? Which mint? The world over there are many varieties of mints and thousands of species of ants, all different in their biologies. When you find an ant colony making a nest in your mint patch you become a skeptic.

Insect populations vary widely from season to season. Other conditions, such as soil and climate, vary too from year to year and place to place. Just introducing new plants into the environment of a garden may provide habitats for insect predators and parasites that were not abundant before. The question is, which exact plant species has which effect on which precise insect? Only a very few cases of this have so far been worked out, in spite of authoritative-sounding lists you may have read that confidently tell you to plant one plant with another to receive a certain result.

The California Highway Landscaping Department is quite progressive in its pest management methods. Through their funding of a biological control project on specific insect pests in certain landscape plants in one part of the state, they have discovered a species of California myrtle that flowers at just the right time of the year to provide nectar and pollen to feed a beneficial insect that will control one of these pest insects. By interplanting California myrtle in strategic areas they solved one of their problems. That is a true case of companion planting being a valid pest management technique. Does that mean that we should recommend the use of California myrtle to you? That would be nonsense, as your insects, soils, climate, and other plants are not the same. However, the idea of providing season-long pollen sources for beneficial insects is an idea probably worth pursuing.

There are unquestionably some plant materials that make effective insect poisons or repellents. Pyrethrins, rotenone (very toxic to fish, by the way), sabadilla, and nicotine (very toxic to man and other mammals) are well-known examples. Catnip seems to have a repellent effect on some insects, and garlic definitely kills larvae of flies and mosquitoes, though little is known about its effects on beneficial insects. We hope to study the effect of these two plant-derived pesticides this coming year.

The point is, however, *none of these plants have their effect just by being present in the garden as companion plants.* All must be ground up and sprayed on the plants to be effective and all may have some of the same disastrous effect on insect populations mentioned earlier in the discussion on pesticides.

Resistant Plants

Many wild plants do contain materials discouraging to insects. These are precisely those bitter oils and alkaloids we have bred out of our cultivated vegetables to obtain the succulent varieties modern consumers tend to prize. Thus many of our cultivated plants are more valuable than their ancestors. Nevertheless, occasionally a variety more resistant to a specific pest insect will be discovered and these can form the basis for a valuable new strain.

Selective breeding like this may be more useful among ornamentals which are not required to be so succulent. When choosing plants from which you plan to save seeds, look for those that might show greater resistance to insect attack than their neighbors.

Resistance to disease has proved a very important characteristic. Many plant varieties have been bred just for this purpose and these are usually well marked in the seed catalogs.

What Should You Do?

When you see wildlife in the garden, enjoy it. If it is an insect, don't worry about whether it is a "good" one or a "bad" one. Ask yourself, "Is it causing intolerable damage?" The same animal may cause problems one year, or in one part of the garden, and may not in another time or place. For example, ants in the soil help to aerate it by making their tunnels and nests. They also kill some soil organisms that can become harmful (like termites). On the other hand, ants running up and down the trunk of a tree protecting aphids or scales from their natural enemies may need to be excluded.

If you do see intolerable damage on a plant, ask yourself, "What is causing it?" It is really easy to be fooled! We found holes in our tomatoes during one season. This became intolerable when every one was damaged just as it was starting to ripen. Then it would shortly begin to rot around the holes. A close look showed a cutworm curled up inside. Nearby, tomato holes housed earwigs and sowbugs. However, a nighttime check with a flashlight showed that slugs were creating the holes and the other animals were merely hiding in them during the day.

Tomatoes have so much foliage, we could easily spare some to a few cutworms. Sowbugs were attracted to the decomposing surface tissues where the tomato had been damaged. Light-shy earwigs, which may nibble on seedlings, are also usefully predacious on plant-eating animals and may cease to be a problem in the vegetable patch once a heavy compost mulch is used.

There were no new holes in the tomatoes once we had handled the slugs with a program of handpicking at night, trapping during the day under overturned flower pots, destroying their habitat (they were breeding under the boards we had set out to walk on, and in a bed of ivy), and surrounding the beds with walks of dry sawdust after every watering or rain. If we hadn't made real efforts to find out the true cause of the holes in the tomatoes we could never have designed an effective management system that would reduce the damage.

When our early spring lettuce was reduced to little nubs, we blamed the slugs. But careful observance at odd hours of the day showed that birds were doing the damage. A series of screen protectors solved that. They stack conveniently out of the way when they aren't needed.

Many animals, including insects, do their damage at

night. Flashlight investigations are sometimes the only way to find out what is really going on. Evening checks will also give you glimpses of beneficial insects, like green and brown lacewings.

When you discover how the damage is occurring, then design a program to *modify the environment* and reduce the population size to the point where you can handle it. Adding flowering plants to the garden so there is a pollen and nectar source for beneficial insects is one way. Protecting predators like predacious ground beetles by giving them a home is another example. We use overturned flow-

cone excluder for the cabbage maggot (seam stapled together)

big screen cage to protect against flies

er pots for this too. Originally we started putting these between the seedlings after uncovering them following transplanting, because our cats would get in there and scratch around in the fresh compost. Then we found the upside-down pots made also good slug traps, ground beetle harborage, and a home for little spiders that would spin their webs across the hole and trap flies that might emerge from the soil where they were pupating.

By studying the animal that is causing problems, one can devise many such methods of managing the habitat that will reduce the pests and favor its natural enemies. Local snakes, toads, spiders, wasps, meat-eating birds (attract them with unsalted suet), all will help in insect control.

The next strategy is *handpicking* of the pests. Aphids can be rubbed off, caterpillars and snails collected; squash bugs and others are easily captured. *Pruning* is also useful in many aphid and caterpillar infestations. Cutting away the areas may not only reduce the population size suddenly, but also remove a favored habitat, as with some aphids that like the inner canopy of certain trees and will not breed in high numbers on the outer branches.

Other important mechanical means are *barriers* and *traps*. We use Stickem to prevent crawling insects from going where we don't want them. Certain honeydew-dripping trees in Berkeley are ringed once a year with a three-inch band of Stickem about eight feet or so off the ground. This prevents ants from ascending and protecting the tree aphids from their natural enemies. Dry sawdust discourages slugs. Screened cages keep out cabbage, carrot, and onion maggots. Although these latter all cause damage to the roots of those vegetables, they are actually the young of flies which can be kept away from the young susceptible plants by a frame barrier of fly screen.

Half a tube from the center of a roll of toilet paper, or a frozen orange juice can with both ends sliced off, makes excellent barriers against cutworms that attack seedlings. After transplanting the young cabbage family plants to the garden, water thoroughly and press the tube down into the softened soil or compost.

Traps are very effective for catching flies. Rolled up newspapers will provide a daytime hiding place for earwigs, if you feel you must catch them. Gophers are best handled by trapping unless you have too small a space; in that case, you can sink a fence of hardware cloth or a cement wall into the ground deep enough to keep them out.

In waiting for natural biological control to have an effect, be patient. The natural enemies of the pest will always lag a little behind, as they must wait for the pest populations to grow sufficiently large to support them. It is common for people to use a pesticide just as the pest population is about to be reduced by natural means. You need to examine insect populations carefully to learn to recognize predators, their eggs, parasitized and diseased insects—all of which will tell you that help is on the way.

One thing should be borne in mind: you always have the option of deciding not to grow a particular plant because constant bug problems make it unsuited to your area.

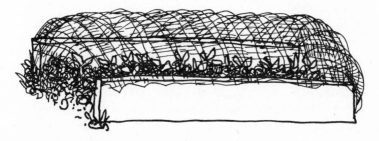

plants protected by chicken wire from hungry birds

Many native plants would make attractive landscaping in places where, instead, people struggle with fragile imported exotics.

When all your alternate methods fail, and you must grow that particular plant, you may wish to resort to the use of some spray. By all means use the least toxic one to man and other vertebrates. Water is the safest. A strong stream is effective in knocking bugs off the plants to the ground where they may be picked up by predators, in breaking up their bodies with its force, and in creating conditions for the spread of insect disease. An old-fashioned fat-based soap may be added to the water to increase wetting power. Green soap, made with potassium stearate (.1 percent solution), is a good one (it can be purchased by writing Michael and Pelton, Emeryville, California). Always test a new material like soap on a portion of the particular plant before using it widely.

There are other nontoxic possibilities, such as diatomaceous earth and silica gel which have an abrasive and drying action upon insects. Dormant oils may be used to smother scales during the period when the plant is not growing actively. One friend of ours successfully used a dilute mixture of sesame oil to control mites on some house plants.

Plants indoors are in such an artificial environment that they may more easily succumb to high pest populations. By putting infested plants outside in a protected spot for a few hours a day during warm weather you may attract the natural enemies of the pest. These frequently cannot be found indoors. Washing house plants with soap and water is another useful technique. Invert the pot, with your hand holding down the soil, and swish the leaves through soapy and then clear water. Mealybugs which may become a problem, particularly when plants get too dry, can often be controlled by applying rubbing alcohol to each one with a small brush.

When caterpillars are the problem you can use B.T., as mentioned earlier in this chapter. It is important to wait until they are large enough to eat both sides of the leaf. A number of failures with this material have resulted from people not realizing that the caterpillar has to ingest the disease spores. If the spray is used when the moths are flying and laying their eggs, or when the caterpillars are so tiny that they are only feeding on one side of the leaf, you will not be successful. B.T. spores will not live in sunlight for more than a short while. If it is applied so that only one side or parts of the leaf are covered (usually the top sides) then the young caterpillars may avoid eating it altogether.

After this in toxicity come pyrethrins, sabadilla, and rotenone—materials which are true poisons not only to some insects but to some other animals, too.

In any case, no matter how safe you feel your particular spray may be, do not use it indiscriminately. Confine its application to *just those specific spots* where the pest population is out of control, so as to preserve as much as possible of the other wildlife that may give you more long-term aid. Remember, insects are wildlife, too.

chapter 11

We Take to the Roof

Container Gardening

Our house, which looks like a castle in front with a circular tower, and has a barn roof tacked on behind, is three stories high. As it sits to the west of our backyard, this means our open ground does not get afternoon sun. The first season we struggled along with leggy broccoli and floppy onions until we finally took the hint. There just wasn't enough sun in our backyard to grow certain things. Lettuce, chard, spinach, carrots, celery, leeks, Jerusalem artichokes, asparagus—they all did fine. But for those vegetables that need more sun, we just had to think of something else.

We took to the roof, the only spot on our property with all-day sun. During the next two years, in an assortment of five-gallon cans, wooden fish boxes, old drawers, and halved thirty- and fifty-gallon drums, we managed to grow large quantities of a variety of vegetables: turnips, beets, zucchini, rutabagas, bell peppers, tomatoes, broccoli, cabbage, cauliflower, and onions.

Container gardening has a great deal to offer city gardeners. Much of the city ground area has been put under concrete for driveways, walks, and patios. Containers of plants allow you to reclaim these spaces. Many city dwellers only rent the property where they live. Growing plants in containers means you don't have to disturb the landlord's landscaping and can take your plants with you when you move.

Containers can be moved around to take advantage of

the changing seasons, also. They can be set under trees, eaves, or on the porch to escape a radiation frost, or even inside when the summer is over. Tomatoes and peppers have both responded to this treatment, in our experience. Plants in high, large, permanent planters, such as we constructed on our porch (out of a set of old garage doors) are easy to reach, weed, and harvest. On the south side of the house, they are perfect for growing early spring vegetables, particularly lettuce. The sun is low in the sky during the winter and slants in under the roof to give the containers plenty of light. But for hot summer middays, the sun is high enough so that the porch roof provides shade. We may be having a heavy spring rain storm, but I can harvest, without getting wet, lettuce for lunch sandwiches or supper salad.

What plants can you grow in containers? That depends on how deep the container is, what sort of light conditions you can provide, and whether you are planning on doing it indoors or outdoors. Herbs and small cherry tomatoes like Tiny Tim can be grown in a six-inch pot inside the house in a sunny window. Certain dwarf citrus can also be grown successfully indoors in large planters. There is an excellent book on how to do this: *Dwarf Fruit Trees, Indoors and Outdoors*, by Robert E. Atkinson (New York, Van Nostrand Reinhold Company, 1972). But ignore the instructions on how to manage insects—it's not necessary to resort to pesticides to handle indoor plants. Handpicking and a few other simple techniques will manage just fine.

Radishes, lettuce, and baby carrots can be grown in soil only six inches deep, but they do better in eight. Eight inches to a foot is better for most other vegetables, too. Tomatoes, broccoli, cucumbers, and zucchini or summer squash will all do much better if they can have one to two feet of depth. In fact, with all of the plants we have tried, the larger the containers, the bigger the harvest. Tomatoes are particularly responsive to root depth. You can prove this for yourself by starting seedlings of a variety of the small cherry tomato, then transplanting one to a six-inch pot, one to a gallon container, another to a five-gallon can, and yet another to an even larger and deeper planter.

In our experience, the plant in the largest container will invariably live the longest and produce the most food. But it is not clear to what extent this is a simple response to greater root space and how much it is due to better nutrition.

As we mentioned in the section on minienvironment, squashes and cucumbers respond well to being grown under conditions where their roots are well fed and watered but their vines are allowed to sprawl over the hot, dry cement of a patio or tarred roof surface. The fact is, all

lettuce in oil
drum cut in half

tomatoes

the vegetables we've raised in containers have done well
and the only common ones we haven't tried that way are
peas, beans, and corn.

Drainage

Regardless of whether your containers are indoors or
out, on the patio or the roof, they share a single important
requirement: good drainage. Plant pathologists have told
us that there has been a noticeable increase in plant disease
since plastic pots have become popular for home and nursery. The best containers are those that breathe, porous
clay (unglazed) being ideal. Wooden containers usually permit some small drainage of water through the cracks between the boards as well as through the drainage holes at
the bottom. We have had good luck with ordinary five-gallon cans, scavenging them from the dumpsters in the industrial section of town and from behind restaurants, but we
are careful to punch drainage holes around the sides at the
very bottom (not in the bottom itself).

You know the hole on the bottom of the flower pot? Do
not put a piece of broken crockery across it. Yes, that is
contrary to what most books say, but we've learned our
methods from an authority on plant disease who has been
called in to diagnose and cure many a sick container-grown
plant. Just firm the dry soil down on the bottom of the
pot. The first time or two you water, a little soil may run
out, but after that it will stabilize itself. He also cautioned
us regarding the practice of putting a layer of stones or
coarse broken pottery in the bottom of a large container.
This will collect water in the spaces thus created and will
not drain properly, again creating conditions favorable for
root disease. Roots will need all available space in the pot,
so avoid the space-filling stones.

If you have a very pretty ceramic container you wish to

use that doesn't have drainage holes in it, use it as the decorative exterior and plant in a smaller pot inside that does have a drainage hole. Set the inner pot on top of some gravel put in the bottom of the outer pot. That way the little pot will not be sitting in water each time you irrigate the plant.

It is very important that plants be watered from the top downward and that they do not sit in the water that has drained through the pot. When this happens, the water rises again by capillary action and then evaporates from the surface of the soil, leaving the salts behind. This is the origin of the white residue often found on the top of the soil around house plants and coating the outside of the clay pot. It is also the cause of house plants turning brown around the edges and tips of the leaves. Probably more house plants are killed by this kind of salt accumulation than anything else that people do to them.

What you should do, if a plant container sits in a saucer so that water can collect below it, is set the pot up on some stones. That way, when the water runs into the saucer it will not touch the bottom of the pot and will not be absorbed up into the soil again. It is also a good idea to allow some water to come out the bottom of the pot to wash accumulated salts through the pot.

For plants where the soil has accumulated excessive salts from improper watering, the best thing is to transplant them into fresh soil and a clean pot. Soak the old salt-encrusted pot in a deep tub or bucket and change the water a couple of times to leach out the salts.

Another aspect of the drainage problem has to do with having a good soil mix in the container. If the basis for your planting mix is clay, as it is with us, then the soil will tend to shrink away from the sides of the container when it dries. The next time you water, you will find the water running over the surface, and down the cracks around the sides between the soil and the container, without thoroughly soaking the earth inside.

For this reason, as well as to make the mixture lighter, it is highly desirable to add a good compost to the planting mix in proportions high enough to keep it porous. There are also commercial materials, sold under various trade names, that can be added to the mix. These will have the same basic effect of improving drainage while paradoxically aiding moisture retention, as the compost does. Vermiculite, which is a commercial expanded mica, has been popular for this purpose, but after a while it starts to break down, with less desirable effects upon the soil mixture. Perlite may be superior for this reason. Frequently these materials are added just in order to obtain a planting mix that does not weigh so much.

If you cannot obtain any soil, but can get waste organic materials with which to make a compost, try planting your vegetables in pure compost. So far we have done this with squash, bush beans, beets and lettuce and in each case have found it equal to or better than the soil compost mix we used before (because it doesn't dry out so fast, is lighter, and provides good nutrition).

The Problems of Weight and Wear

When we decided to roof garden, our first requirement was to protect the surface of the roof itself. Ours was covered with a heavy weight (ninety-pound) tar paper. On top of this we built a skeleton of a wood platform to support our containers, with solid boards for walkways in between.

What we worried about most was weight. A cubic foot of water weighs approximately sixty-two pounds: this has to be taken into account. Since the main walls of the house were sturdy, but the roof frame itself was not built to take any weight, we located the containers around the edges of the roof and used our wooden platform to distribute the weight between containers. We also went to some lengths to make the soil mix as light as possible.

We used approximately 1/3 perlite, 1/3 compost, mixed with 1/3 soil, and have had to take special precautions to fertilize these containers regularly. We found rabbit manure a good mulch, along with compost for the top of the containers. Watering with dilute urine (and the addition of a little lime) is a good idea also. Still lighter mixes have been developed for container-grown plants. But, as they usually contain only varying proportions of peat moss, sand, and perlite, they must be fertilized entirely by additions of some sort. Peat moss, in spite of being an organic material, contributes almost no nutrients to the mix. Without organic matter, of course, they cannot support populations of animals and microorganisms that would decompose them to a form the plant roots can take advantage of.

Since our mixes contain abundant compost and soil right from our yard (we took soil from a particularly good area beneath a cherry plum, where leaves had been accumulating for many a year), the plants have lots of nutrients. We were also careful to introduce earthworms to every container.

Spacing of the vegetables in the larger containers turns out to be rather similar to growing them in the ground. Although, in general, we tend to grow our plants a lot closer together than many standard works on the subject suggest. I can only conclude that these works are written with mechanized agriculture in mind, or at least assuming cultivation with a plow. If in doubt, plant close and thin as the seedlings get crowded.

Weeding and watering both seemed particularly easy on

the roof, although the containers dried out much more quickly than the soil in the yard. Our insect visitors seemed much the same as down below, though it was easier to come out at night for handpicking forays against cutworms. We had fewer problems with slugs and snails, which are great pests in our area generally, having been

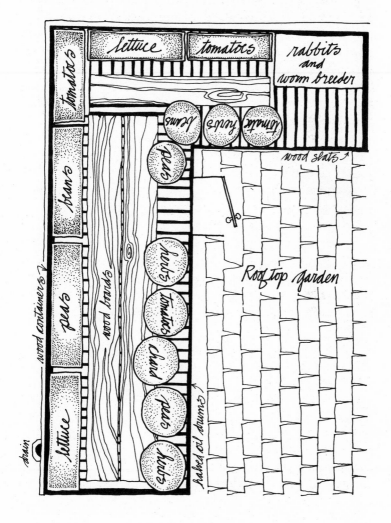

introduced from Europe without their natural predators and parasites. It may be that, since they do not fly, they rarely discovered that anything edible was up there.

The single difference in growing food on the roof that we really had to deal with was the amount of wind. Plants that normally do not need support, such as sprouting broccoli and eggplant, did better firmly tied to a stake. We also anchored down the compost mulch with burlap pieces, tucked in at the edges or weighted down by overturned pots or stones—all just to prevent the mulch from being blown away and the soil surface from drying out.

A Meat and Greens System

We are continuing to experiment with this rooftop system as this book is being written. Our scheme is to show how some food raising may be introduced even into the heart of an urban area, such as downtown San Francisco. Such city centers often have residences mixed in with light industrial establishments. The people living in these narrow alley-like ghettos usually have no spot of ground to garden in or even much sunlight for a window box because of the several-story buildings on all sides. But the area seen from a tall building nearby provides a vista of flat roof after roof, all soaking up the sun, doing nothing but increasing the temperatures of the city.

Our plan is to show how meat rabbits can be raised on such roofs and fed primarily from the wastes of the local grocery stores. Their manure could be processed right there by manure worms, or made into compost, and the results turned into containers which would then be used to grow some salad vegetables. This system theoretically could provide a fair amount of food in a small area, with the only continuous inputs from outside the system being sawdust, vegetable scraps, a small amount of alfalfa pellets for the pregnant doe rabbits and babies, and occasional additions of lime—none of which would be expensive. There would need to be some initial investments: lumber and wire to build the system, although some of this could be scrap scavenged from waste bins in the area, peat moss as bedding for the worms, perlite for the planter boxes, and the cost of the starting pair of rabbits and the worms. We have all of these components going already, and all we need is further experimentation to integrate them all into a single unit on the roof, and to determine the costs and profits of such a system.

We know that people tend to be very conservative regarding their food habits, and many otherwise voracious consumers of meat become all sentimental and filled with what we call the "Bambi" syndrome when they think of eating rabbit. Adoption of such a new system requires assimilating some additional information: how to raise rabbits, butcher them, tan the pelts, cook the meat, etc. The success of our scheme may depend more on changing the cultural prejudices of people than on the real feasibility of the system as a way to introduce food production into downtown city roof areas.

chapter 12

How About a Community Garden?

Once our urban farm was under way, it attracted the attention of a great many people. We would show our friends around, then they would send their friends to have a look. The neighbors began to arrange tours for *their* friends. Our students would bring other students at odd hours of the day. We would hear voices outside the window while eating breakfast and look up to find a train of complete strangers walking by, oohing and aahing, poking and peering at things. It was rather like living in a fish bowl.

We were beginning to worry about soil compaction. When five people get into our yard at the same time it seems crowded! This was becoming a steady stream of visitors, klomping through our strawberries and leaping over the chard. One day the doorbell rang, and there was a nice couple from Massachusetts who were on a trip across the country. They had heard about our little city food-growing venture and thought they'd drop in.

That was the last straw. It was either start selling tickets or move some of our food-raising activities to a more public place and regain some privacy at home.

If one of our motives in growing our own food was to pass on the information to others, then we needed to find a setting in which to do this. Raising our own food in a public place would mean for every hour of time and energy we put into it, we could affect hundreds rather than dozens of people. So we started the student garden at the Oxford Tract of the University of California in Berkeley, and the rooftop project with our Antioch College/West students.

These two projects are open to the public, and occasionally nonstudents participate in them. However, they are not truly public gardens. Such community vegetable plots would be a really good addition to American urban areas, and a few towns are beginning to realize it. In every city there are apartment dwellers who don't have land to garden in and renters whose landlords don't like the idea of tearing up the lawn to grow food. At the same time there are many waste spaces, publicly or commercially owned, as well as park areas with ornamental plantings that are mistreated by the local residents because they don't feel a meaningful connection to the land or the city government. In short, there are many city people who could be interested in growing their own food and many suitable places in urban areas that might be used for such ventures.

With people from Ecology Action in Berkeley who were also interested in encouraging a city-wide movement to use empty lots for neighborhood food raising, we approached the Parks and Recreation Department of Berkeley. Walter Toney, the superintendent, was enthusiastic, and we began a survey of the suitable areas. We requested city support to install water outlets and build fences to keep out dogs and vandals, and also to join us in recommending to owners (many of them absentee) that their lots be used for this purpose.

Before the project went very far, we found out that the fire department was spraying vacant lots with herbicides. In some cases they used Simazine, a long-lasting poison. Although supposedly it penetrates only a few inches into the ground and only lasts for about six months, tests in our class at the university showed that, in some areas at least, it actually penetrated more than six inches and lasted over a year. This was being done "to prevent fires" during the summer when the rain does not normally fall in our area.

This use of herbicides had to be stopped before food

raising could begin on those vacant lots, and it finally was. It took time, an aroused group of people to exert political pressure, the proper information, and the suggestion of an alternative—using fire-retardant plants in some places and cultivation in others. Along the way we discovered that activated charcoal, when turned into the soil at 300 pounds per acre, could help reduce the effect of the Simazine.

The vacant lot project still hasn't gotten off the ground in Berkeley, but it has a good chance of doing so in the future because of the encouraging attitude of the city personnel, the general interest of the population, and the rising food prices. In the meantime, we have been able to help a couple of other garden projects get started, by an Oakland black community school, the Junior League, and many other groups and individuals.

A California based group, The Institute of Self-Reliance, has been successful in organizing regular classes in food-producing skills for urban and suburban people. They teach vegetable gardening, small animal raising, home orchard care, and food preservation, using a practical yet very scientific and environmentally sound approach. We have been helping them out whenever possible in establishing community teaching gardens and developing courses in instruction.

From these experiences we have learned a number of things we'd like to pass on to you. First of all, if the land does not belong to the people doing the gardening, obtain in writing an agreement regarding its use, and the minimum length of time it will be available. Secondly, find individual people who will take responsibility for either the entire project or significant parts of it, such as composting, starting seeds, watering, wildlife management, providing reliable information for the participants and visitors, and controlling the behavior of visitors. This last can usually be done by constructing prominent walkways and putting up signs warning people to stay off the beds, keep out dogs, hang on to their toddlers, etc. A sandbox to one side, with a tub of water, is one thing that will keep the little ones busy while adults are visiting or working in the garden.

Another highly appreciated feature of the gardens we have been associated with is the educational display developed for identifying vegetables, weeds, and bugs, giving recipes for lesser-known edibles, describing our compost system, and so forth. Whenever we have had the budget, we have made available hand-out sheets, many of which have become an integral part of this book.

Sign-up sheets for jobs a week ahead, a file with names and phone numbers of all participants, a surrounding fence, a first-aid kit, a locked tool box with the combination known only to key workers, and a shady place to sit and admire what you've done, have all been important components of the systems with which we've been involved.

Perhaps the most valuable advice we can give you, besides finding a responsible individual or a small group of committed people who will take responsibility for parts of the project, is: *start small!* Build your compost system first and have that going smoothly before you start to plant. Don't spade up the whole area at once, but rather develop it bed by bed by adding compost as it becomes available. A small, gorgeously successful plot is far more rewarding than a large, back-breaking, woebegone-looking one. If individuals and families are to have control over separate plots, rather than everyone gardening together, then have someone coordinate the overall management of the composting and the communicating of reliable information to everyone.

We found that the biggest problem with our public compost system was people excited over the idea of recycling who were eager to bring us their kitchen garbage. We discouraged this unless they were also willing to participate in the making and the turning of the compost too. This was partly because the people who do the actual work of the composting always have enough kitchen wastes of their own, but mainly because we are not interested in becoming garbage collectors for others. Our real interest is in getting people to confront their *own* wastes and to learn how to handle them. A community garden, coordinated by one or more competent persons, is an ideal way to teach those necessary skills.

In general, food producing is so pleasant a recreation with such obvious rewards for stomach and spirit, that we can conceive of no finer vision than each community in the United States emulating those European towns that provide public gardening space, rented for a small fee each year to pay for maintaining the boundaries and providing water. Each plot has its own tool shed and a small cabana for shade and relaxation, where whole families may go to engage in some pleasant physical labor and provide themselves with a goodly portion of each week's food.

chapter 13

Confessions of
Two Crazy Environmentalists

We began our urban farm with the goal of raising our own food free of pesticides, hormones, preservatives, artificial flavors, and dyes. We did just this for a great deal of our food right where we live, in the city of Berkeley, California. We learned a lot and hope what is recorded here will be of use to others. We believe that what we created with our own life styles has already influenced other city residents. We've met a lot of fine people doing the same, and we expect to meet many more. What we would like to do with this last chapter is suggest an overall scheme for further expansion on the theme of "Raising Food in the City." Possibly each of us can take on developing a small portion of the entire plan from which will grow another larger conception for human life.

First we need to discuss long-term survival strategies, then applications with specific suggestions, including urban agriculture, and then some ideas about what the future possibilities are.

Long-Term Survival
Strategies

Two basic sources of energy are currently being used: they are solar and fossil. By solar I mean the energy captured by green plants that is ultimately used by man for food, fiber, and structures. The other is the fossil energy sources or the mining and petrochemical group. Here the ultimate source is also the sun, but with a large gap of time between when the earth was formed from the sun and when plant and animal life was converted to fossilized sources of oil and natural gas.

Another basic difference between the two sources is that the solar path is renewable but the fossil is not. This means essentially that once the fossil supplies are used up there will be no more, but that the renewable supplies can be produced as long as the sun shines. With some careful thought we can see that modern industrialized society now depends largely on fossil supplies of raw materials for fuels, textiles, plastics, lubricants, minerals, fertilizers, pesticides, rubbers, dyes, pigments, flavors, perfumes, and medicines.

The future is easy to read, knowing these facts. As the supplies of fossil nutrients dwindle, the cost of extracting the materials will increase; as these costs increase, the price of all the processes that depend on them will also increase. Since most of the materials of our society depend upon these basic supplies, all products will increase in price. This in turn will again affect the extraction costs and still again, across the board, the costs of all derived goods and materials.

The most critical industry affected by all these rising costs will be the agriculture-food industry. This can already be seen in rising food prices. An example of how this works is very instructive. Consider that current-day agriculture is basically operated by machinery which requires fuels, oils, and lubricants, besides a lot of maintenance. It's simple to see that food costs will rise when fuel costs increase, because the producers will merely push the greater costs onto the consumer. The rise, however, will be compounded because fuel is used at many points along the way to your table.

Today's agriculture uses energy to till the soil and shape

the beds, inject fertilizer, irrigate, apply herbicides, fungicides, and insecticides, harvest, and transport to market. Thus, if the cost of each of these processes goes up, the total cost of crop production goes up accordingly. Since it also takes fuels and energy costs to process, store, pack, and ship, and then it also takes fuel to go to the store, shop, and bring the food home, store, and prepare it, it is easy to see how food prices will increase drastically from merely a small increase in fuel costs.

A full picture of what is in store for us can easily be seen when one considers that food is the fuel of humanity. Since humans rely on other humans for education, health care, legal and other services, one can see that the costs of these services will increase as the fuel (food) for maintaining these service specialists also increases. Again there is a multiplying effect since all the services require special equipment and structures to support such service people.

The future with such a view looks bleak but is bleaker still since we know that the population is still growing, which means more food is needed. The urbanization of excellent farm land is not helping the food supply problem either. By building on some of the best agricultural lands in the world, here in California, farmers are forced to increase yields and bring poorer-grade soils into production. Using poorer soils requires more energy because more fertilizer, water, and management are needed.

The full picture of the problems ahead of us includes not only scarcity and the economic ramifications of having less energy, minerals, agricultural and wild lands, but also a reduction in the quality of our living experience. This is already being felt in smoggy skies, crowded cities, increased noise levels, etc. What few people are willing to face, however, is that the basic ingredients of life-support, the quality of air, water, and food, have undergone a transformation in the last twenty years the scope of which is difficult to fully comprehend.

In 1970, fifty million tons of synthetic chemicals were produced in the United States. These chemicals are incorporated in our clothing, dishes, soaps, toothbrushes and toothpaste, shampoos, deodorants, eyeglasses, and are found also in the car, the garage, the kitchen, the yard, and living room—in short, everywhere. Not knowing what these synthetic chemicals are only makes the problems of managing the toxic members of this large group more difficult.

The use of pesticides illustrates how pervasive and monstrous only one facet of this larger problem is. In 1970 some 900 registered pesticides, totaling nearly a billion pounds, were used in the United States. These 500,000 tons of poison are mistakenly believed to be directed at about 200 "pest" plants, microbes, and animals. In reality, these substances fall on entire ecosystems and frequently become circulatory poisons in the planet's larger cycles.

Pesticides are routinely found in large numbers of food chains, probably including the entire human food web, drinking water, in all major waterways in the United States, in the oceans, in the air and soil throughout the world. Information about production of genetic defects and cancers is only gradually being discovered *after the fact*, frequently after world-wide exposure.

Yesterday's newspaper had an article about spraying a poison called furadan on 364,000 acres of alfalfa. A piece of news like that usually means furadan may start showing up in milk or beef or cheese, because alfalfa is fed in large measure to cattle. But here is the important point: you will not know about it! You will take it into your body along with a whole host of other things as long as you buy at the local supermarket.

We hope the view of the world through our pesticide-colored glasses has frightened you. It frightens us, but it also moved us toward producing our own food. The fact that a hormone, DES, was incorporated into our meat led us toward producing our own meat. It also undermined our confidence in our food industry to such an extent that we learned what it would take to produce more of our own. We are convinced that a great many others can also produce a significant portion of their own diet, and we created this book to help you to make the first steps toward doing the same. Here also are some reasons why urban food production or urban agriculture, as we call it, is important.

Urban Agriculture: Reasons Why

1. By converting ornamental plantings, yards, vacant lots, and other urban spaces into areas where food can be produced, the impact of the population-land squeeze can be reduced and once-productive soils can again support people.

2. By developing food-producing systems close to where the food will be consumed, a basic flaw in modern civilization can be corrected: the urban-rural separation.

3. Home food production can bring about an awakening of interest in the earth, plants, animals, and nature study that can dismantle the consumptive and apathetic urban life style.

4. By scattering small, intensive, diversified food-producing units throughout cities and suburbs, more small-scale, stable insect communities can be produced, requiring fewer pesticides for management—possibly none.

5. By creating viable examples for people to learn from and elaborate on, more people will take control of their own life-support processes. This could create an informed, active citizenry that can produce healthy changes in our civilization.

6. By learning and practicing gardening, composting, and animal husbandry, more people can become awar. of the great power in natural systems and the survival potential in harmonizing human life support with the planet's processes.

7. By creating and managing your own life-support systems, you can learn by proxy what it will take to manage the entire human life-support system.

8. By discovery and study of the bountiful animals of the soil and garden, you can regain a knowledge of the paths through which man has passed and will continue to pass.

9. By taking one step toward self-support and by learning that all actions affect all other actions, you can begin to understand how individual action can change the world. Finally, you may even think about a great new civilization.

10. By individuals learning, discovering, building, and relearning, the steps for building a new solar civilization, where the essentials of life will be produced directly from plant products, can be accomplished. The home and family unit may again become a basic cornerstone of a planetary civilization.

Life-Style Changes

A life style is a person's way of life. If you move one step toward recycling, using less energy and fewer materials for life support, you have started to change your life style. The processes grow on you. We started with a compost system and a garden, later added rabbits and chickens, then ate from rooftop gardens, tried growing mushrooms, and later, when the traffic from visitors got to be too much, developed a teaching community garden in the middle of Berkeley. Methane generators were next, then we changed the city's pest control program (to decrease pesticides on the leaves used in our compost, and to increase the survival of beneficial insects), and are now planning for fish, wind, and solar systems, as well as others. This has been our approach; you can try another. Here are some suggestions:

All efforts to readjust the life-support system fall into two general groups: 1) new creations or old adaptations, and 2) reducing needs. The first group is more glamorous and probably more exciting, but the second group is probably more effective. Some examples of the second group may clarify the point.

When we used to boil a cup of water, first we'd get the pot, fill it up well beyond the needed one cup, set it on the stove, and wait. After a while we'd hear the water boil and go pour a cup of tea or coffee. Now we rarely bother with tea or coffee, but drink herb teas we grow ourselves, fill the pot only for as many cups as we will actually need, and turn off the heat as soon as the water is hot enough. The overall result of such attention to details is a different approach to using resources. Such efforts are more difficult to achieve for some people than buying or making a new energy source, because of the way we think about things. This example could be expanded to include walking and using a bicycle or train instead of the automobile, a phone call or note instead of a trip by car, and in general a less material-resource-use approach to living. Obviously one still needs to use resources to live, but by starting to work on ourselves, we can use less of them.

We have learned that chickens like to eat greens, particularly grass clippings. Here's a story about people and a status symbol that has a practical slant after a social statement.

Lawns: "What for Art Thou?"

A student of ours, while living in San Francisco, happened to look up from her books one sunny afternoon and saw a gardener pull up in front of a city residence in his truck. What she saw is probably being repeated millions of times every day throughout the industrialized nations. Now, it turns out the gardener was only out to take care of the lawn. It also turns out that the lawn was only what we call a postage stamp lawn—you know, four by four. Hardly big enough for one person to sit on, yet enough to need a gardener, since the people who live in the house do not have the time or inclination to take care of a lawn.

The story is really about what the gardener did. First, he took out a small machine that looked like an eggbeater that has been squashed. This, we've learned since, is an edger. By pulling a rope it starts up and is used to cut the edges of the lawn. Then a lawn mower followed with its usual cloud of smoke, noise, and spew of grass. The final machine is a blower—here modern man has surely come of age! This machine is strapped to the back of the gardener and used to blow the unorderly clippings produced from the previous process back onto the lawn or other areas where they will not appear unsightly.

After a short bit of clipping with a hand-type scissor object, the man loads up, leaps into his truck, and is off. The whole process took about fifteen to twenty minutes, and when our student related the story to us, she was holding her sides at the humor of so much ado about nothing (or very little). The story stuck in our minds because it says so much about what kind of civilization we have created and what kind of lives people live.

The whole story about lawns is not, however, contained in this brief scenario. Lawns, to the best of our knowledge, were created as a status symbol originally by pastoral people who could display to their neighbors the fact that they had some pasture on which they didn't need to graze an animal. Today the tradition has been passed down to us, including, besides the smoke, noise, and fuel expenditure (all in place of hand-operated machines), whole shelves of herbicides, fungicides, and insecticides. Notwithstanding their environmental impact, including the fact that they could be better made into fuels, with less poison circulating in ourselves, our food, and our wildlife, the final product—the grass—*is thrown away*! To bring sanity to this situation, we encourage people to use the harvest by feeding it to chickens or rabbits, and if this is not possible, to put it in the compost. It has a great deal of nitrogen in its leaves and it is already cut up. Lawn grasses are very productive. A word of caution: avoid grass that has been treated with any pesticide, particularly if you are using it as an animal feed. If you are using it in the compost, especially an aerobic compost, some pesticides can be taken apart by the heat and organisms, but not the chlorinated hydrocarbons like DDT, chlordane, lindane, dieldrin, endrin, and still others. These poisons probably all accumulate in food chains, which is why all pesticide-treated grass should be avoided.

The final question about what lawns really are depends upon who you are. They can be feed for fowl or a fouling place for men. Possibly by raising chickens and feeding them grass, you too will see the value in the grass we waste.

The Future

Obviously, if enough people all put their attention to developing small-scale life-support systems, a great many of the problems involved in developing such systems will be solved. Signs of such developments are already appearing. Last week in the newspaper we saw that an architect nearby has designed two homes to be powered by a wind-mill so that when no power from the wind or storage batteries is available, power from the electric company will be switched on automatically. Obviously this is a step in the right direction, but this example is useful in pointing out some important points about future direction for self-sufficiency enthusiasts. Some of these points are best ap-proached by considering certain statements about design.

1. Focus design efforts on systems that can be built, rebuilt, repaired and maintained by yourself.

2. In designing systems, use materials which can be grown or produced yourself.

3. Concentrate design activities on constructing a life style that uses the smallest amounts of energy and material resources.

4. Do not look for the utopian society, but rather transi-tional forms that can be implemented with slight increases in knowledge and skills.

5. Seek knowledge upon which to build a new civiliza-tion from the old—there's no need to destroy, only trans-form.

6. Discover how other civilizations used plants and plant products and adapt them for small-scale use.

7. Look at and discover how to use waste products.

8. Become aware of toxic materials and learn to avoid contact with them.

9. Seek and develop alternative systems for living and producing the necessities of life.

Why Crazy?

Why do we say "crazy" environmentalists? The answer is a little complex. When we started experimenting with ur-ban farming, we saw our lives change. We saw first our physical environment change, as old things were used in new ways. Five containers appeared under the sink: one for plastics, one for paper to be burned and later recycled, one for metal, and a fourth for glass to be taken to the recycling center, and an organic bucket for composting. Later we saw milk cartons stacking up for planting trays, and still later compost materials accumulated and were transformed into fertilizer. There were many other changes as well.

All this action was fun, exciting, and productive, like pioneering in a place where few have tried before. When our friends came to visit or called, we showed them what we were doing, and since it was different from what they were doing, sometimes we appeared to have changed very much. When you get enough peculiar looks and then wonder why all these other people aren't producing their own food, you think about words like "crazy" to describe either us or them.

It may be useful to give some specific examples of areas where we think urban agriculture needs development, starting with the home. A new integration between garden, composting, and animal systems, harvesting, preparing, storage, and eating areas can be created that makes it easier to move materials from seed to plate. New systems which we will probably work on in the future include seed storage and retrieval, greenhouse, mushrooms, feed mixing and preparation. Next comes adapting animal products like fur, skins, feathers, and silkworm cocoons for clothing.

An integration of agricultural systems and architectural innovations in the home is also needed. These include waste management (methane digester and composting), solar driers and heaters, wind generators, and pumps. Fish and algal systems have already been started, but you can see that there is easily the work of many lifetimes here. Possibly you can join us and start to work on yourself and your place.

Index